DANCES
with
SPIRITS

ANCIENT WISDOM FOR A MODERN WORLD

CALVIN HELIN

ISBN: 978-1-62467-171-5 (print)
ISBN: 978-1-62467-170-8 (epub)
ISBN: 978-1-62467-267-5 (epdf)

PREMIER PUBLISHING

Published by Premier Digital Publishing
www.premierdigitalpublishing.com
Follow us on Twitter @PDigitalPub
Follow us on Facebook: Premier Digital Publishing

CONTENTS

To my lifelong mentor and good friend Greg Millbank and his wife Fong
for providing me with the opportunity to receive an education
and for teaching me that the kingdom of knowledge is immeasurably
more valuable than a kingdom of riches.

ACKNOWLEDGMENTS

I would like to acknowledge the specific support of my mother, Sigyidm hana'a Su Dalx (Verna Helin), and father, Sm'ooygit Nees Nuugan Noos (Barry Helin), whose collective love and encouragement have allowed me to do what I love to do—write. I also wish to recognize the general support of John and Inez Helin, Pat and Barb Helin, Elaine Hughes, Ramona Crosby, Crystal Leask, Te Taru White, Italia Gandolfo, and Bruce and Elaine (Gosselin) Falstead.

Contemplating Cosmic Grace
(The author at about age three, circa 1963)

SPIRIT DANCER

Found the song
Lost the tune.
No midnight tango
In winter moon.

Out of sync
With cosmic drum.
Samba awaits
Summer sun.

Finding balance
Harmonic choir.
Flamenco wants
A hot fall fire.

With heart free
Let passion soar.
Spirit dances
To spring's roar.

PREFACE

We are not human beings on a spiritual journey.
We are spiritual beings on a human journey.

—PIERRE TEILHARD DE CHARDIN

$\mathcal{I}$ was first touched by the amazing grace of nature as a small boy in my hometown of Lax Kw'alaams (formerly Port Simpson), a remote indigenous British Columbia community on the edge of the fertile coastal temperate rainforest. Human habitation on the ancestral tribal lands of the Tsimshian dates back 13,000 years.[1] In 1834, a Hudson's Bay Company fort was established, attracting a significant Tsimshian resident population, a community that grew into the center for the Northwest Coast in that period.

The village I grew up in contained some of the coast's finest Victorian homes. My mother, Sigyidim hana'a Su Dalx (Verna Helin), recalls visiting her grandmother in the beautiful old mansion known locally as the "Eagle House."[2] A house of comparable pedigree was purchased by my father, Smo'ooygit Nees Nuugan Noos (Chief Barry Helin), for the princely sum of $500. It turned out that our palatial but decrepit dwelling had at one time been the post office for the community. Though the house was grand, our family's financial means were not. We were so poor when we moved in that I can remember our kitchen chairs were roughly hewn blocks of wood, and our table was a bigger block of wood with a circular piece of plywood nailed to the top of it. Our modest financial resources were not of too much concern since fish and game were in abundant supply. As children, my siblings and I felt privileged to live in that dignified historic dwelling filled with the echoes of another time and in the midst of awe-inspiring natural surroundings.

Often in the morning when it was sunny on our back porch, while bathing in the sun's warming rays, I would sit quietly and peacefully absorbing the majesty of nature. Listening to the sweet cadences of the gently babbling brook that ran behind our house, I could watch the sunlight dance on its undulating ripples. Occasionally, a soft breeze would whisper through the leaves of the salmonberry, Devil's club, and salal bushes that surrounded our backyard. The morning dew would twinkle with little bursts of light on alder leaves, cedar fronds, and dance on pine and spruce needles—turning nature's luxuriant blanket that encircled our backyard into a stage set. I would listen to the evocative symphony of the salmonberry bird,[3] the sweet chirping of robins,[4] and the melodious calls of chickadees[5] twittering to a glorious new morning. (My dad's good friend "Uncle Walter" used to say that the chickadees were singing "my tummy's sore.") Chiming in occasionally would be the coarse cawing of crows and hoarse, croaking sound of ravens, interrupted every now and then by the raucous and cheeky "shack, shack, shack" calls of Steller's jays[6] in the distance.

Eagle House in Lax Kw'alaams
(belonged to author's maternal great grandmother)

There I would sit, a small boy, intoxicated by the sensuous and splen-diferous beauty of nature—truly a paradise on earth. Right there, being little me and part of everything else all at once—just outside our back door. These simple, enriching experiences were priceless—yet they didn't cost a cent.

Later, poverty taught my family lessons of frugality. My father and his brothers, all commercial fishermen, earned a living in the winter by tearing down old fish canneries. Additionally, my father took the opportunity to salvage an enormous amount of waste lumber, which was piled about 20 feet high all over our yard. The job of my older brothers and me was to remove all the nails from the lumber and restack the wood in organized piles. The nails were thrown into an empty 45-gallon drum and had to be straightened for reuse—a recycling strategy that saved trees and a host of related packaging and shipping expenses.

My reverie also hearkens back to indigenous ancestors and their com-munion with nature in ancient times, when hearts were more open to the elements. It was a time when people would speak to the animals, to the mountains, to the stars like the innocent children they were; a time when these aspects of nature would, in turn, whisper their secrets; a time when spirituality was not a concept but deeply ingrained in life; a time when people were attuned to the rhythms of the cosmos; a time when people's hearts, thoughts, words, and actions were in harmony; a time of comparatively peaceful social order—even if aspects of material life were often harsh. Today, I shudder to realize how distant we have become from experiencing such connection to nature, such spiritual grace, and such social harmony.

Sadly, today, what we see throughout modern society are people under constant stress yearning for a life with greater meaning and a healthier social environment. We seem to have forgotten that we are simply citizens of nature. Spiritual and social fulfillment, the wellspring that nourishes our emotional well-being, are being woefully neglected. This trend is abetted by a Western worldview that supports an economic system that pushes us along at an ever-increasing frenetic pace while focusing our time and attention on the spiritually empty quest of materialism and consumption, denying the majority of citizens more fulfilling social pursuits.

Modern people, storming along in the digital age, would be well served to remember the values and perspectives of indigenous North American and other ancient cultures. It is particularly important that we adopt wiser courses of action and behavior when the available technology and Western lifestyles have the capacity to wreak so much havoc on the well-being of people and their most fundamental social structures—not to mention the potential of destroying the very planet on which we live.

In seeking the wisdom of the past for solutions to the social and spiritual problems of the present—in participating in "dances with spirits"—we should remember that wisdom to find a path of action for a constructive way forward; we must discover how to find a balance between the valuable material and technological gifts of modern society and the prudent attitudes and behaviors that guided our ancestors. This unquestionably means going beyond the kinds of shallow Western Eurocentric thinking that got us into such dire states in the first place.

In our search for greater harmony, we should be mindful of the lesson that I learned as a small boy—that we do not really need much in a material way to be happy and to experience fulfillment in a deeply peaceful manner. In the spiritual and social realms, once we have provided for our basic needs and attained a reasonably comfortable lifestyle, less is definitely more.

In preparation for discovering wisdom of the past that can help inspire our way forward, we must take a deep breath and step back from our hectic pace, while remembering the kindness and resolve that our grandparents brought to their lives. We must want to live in "the right way" as the ancient chiefs would have advised, being of good heart, clear thought, and honorable action. With this truly sacred inquiry in mind, I bow my head and begin this book, as indigenous people begin everything—with the following prayer:

A PRAYER

O Great Spirit
Seek your light.
Humble being
Wanting sight.

Morning dew
Sparkling stream.
Vision quest
Shaman's dream.

Puny being
Weak and frail.
Without love
Doldrums sail.

Twinkling star
Harvest moon.
An open heart
Mystic's tune.

Mighty soul
Path I seek.
Wisdom's muse
Poet's speak.

Blade of grass
Whispering pine.
Sipping nature's
Holy wine.

Summer breeze
Winter chill.
Standing strong
Unbending will.

Divine Creator
At your feet.
With nature's love
Myself to beat.

Humility's tears
Soak the soil.
With humble heart
I will toil.

Wise Grandfathers
Bless my path.
With sacred tears
In hallowed bath.

Crazy Horse Seeks Vision

INTRODUCTION

A very great vision is needed, and the man who has it must
follow it as an eagle seeks the deepest blue of the sky.

—**TASHUNKEWITKO (CRAZY HORSE), OGLALA**

*W*e live in a society where people enjoy more leisure time, have more
political and economic choices, experience greater personal liberties, and
can use technology to solve more problems than ever before. By many in-
dicators, such as longevity, quality of healthcare, and material living stan-
dards, life clearly appears to be better than in the past.

However, the light that has illuminated this "progress" also casts a long
and terrible shadow. On the heels of a century-long party of materialism,
we face an unexpected economic, spiritual, and social hangover that is
causing pervasive misery. Our society emphasizing instant gratification,
competition, and conspicuous consumption leading to narcissism also
tends to promote social isolation. From this has emerged a society fraught
with loneliness, uncertainty, growing anxiety, a widespread sense of dispir-
ited purposelessness, and accelerating despondency. Comfort is frequently
sought in a bottle of booze, in prescription and illegal drugs, or in a host
of vacuous, time-wasting entertainment distractions, diversions that fail to
fill the social and spiritual void.

Perhaps it is time to acknowledge the dysfunction of the status quo so
that we can take constructive steps to replenish long-neglected spiritual,
moral, and social longings. It is clear we crave and need experience that
supports our innate qualities as social and spiritual animals requiring a
sense of belonging and self-worth.

In thinking about the economic, social, and spiritual problems in to-
day's Western societies, I am reminded of my experience as an adolescent
reading the book *Ishi in Two Worlds* about a man named Ishi, the last mem-
ber of a now extinct Native American tribe who became renowned as "the

last wild Indian in North America." Ishi's story began on August 9, 1911, when he was captured in the corral of a slaughterhouse near the small town of Oroville, California. After Ishi's grandmother and sister had been killed by settlers several years earlier, he wandered alone in the wilderness, not speaking to anyone. Subsequently, he ended up in the Hearst Museum in San Francisco, the anthropology museum of the University of California, where he worked as a janitor. In his brief lifetime, he bridged the huge gulf between so-called Stone Age people and twentieth-century culture.[1]

Ishi was from a tribe of people known as the Yahi, who were located 60 miles north of what is now Sacramento, California. Ishi was the last surviving member of the Yahi tribe, who were systematically exterminated by local vigilante cattlemen after being displaced from their traditional territories as their tribal lands were granted to settlers following the pattern of European settlement that occurred throughout America. The settlers, fixed with common Eurocentric misconceptions about indigenous people, perpetuated the myth of the Yahi as plunderers, murderers, and savages. What they did not understand was how their encroachment in Yahi territories had displaced traditional food sources of the Yahi. Like any people desperate to survive, the Yahi were simply taking what they needed in periods of starvation when the only course open to them was to raid provisions and stock of the settlers.

It was learned later from Ishi how gentle, reserved, patient, and determined they were—how they endured the most horrifying ordeal with the utmost grace. While his tribe existed, they led a lifestyle that, while materially and technologically deficient, was socially and spiritually uplifting—truly a kinder, gentler existence during an era when people had more time and took more care.

It was interesting to me to imagine what Ishi thought about the "progress" of Western industrial culture of the time. Observant and analytical, he was reluctant to voice such an opinion because to criticize anyone so directly was considered to be terrible manners—even if it involved the Europeans who had exterminated his family and tribe. However, Ishi did

Ishi between Two Worlds

reluctantly admit that he ". . . considered the whiteman to be fortunate, inventive and very, very clever . . . however . . . *child-like, lacking in desirable reserve, and in true understanding of Nature . . .*"[2] [Emphasis added] He was also said to have thought of Europeans ". . . as sophisticated children— *smart but not wise* knowing many things, and much that is false . . . but not knowing nature which is always true."[3] [Emphasis added]

Since reading the account of Ishi's life as a young boy, I often contemplated what he really meant in saying that Europeans were "clever . . . but not very wise." After reflecting on this, I think he was commenting on his perceived view of the impact that modern life had on people and nature. Despite the abundance of material possessions and the ongoing technological "cleverness," this society does not seem to be leading to beneficial social and spiritual circumstances for ordinary people, where individuals feel loved, valued, and part of a larger, more satisfying social order. In addition, the fundamental building blocks of organized human society—the family and the community, and their spiritual needs—are under constant siege for being inadvertently at odds with a technologically driven economic system that has very different priorities than the holistic well-being of people.

Given the impact of modern society on the existing population and environment, more attention ought to be paid to the concerns expressed by Ishi and similar ancestral wisdom found in all cultures. This is particularly true when many individuals are seriously questioning how much longer we can perpetuate a lifestyle that takes a high toll on human health, happiness, and the cultural and physical environment—especially at a time when evidence of an imminent economic and environmental collapse is becoming harder to ignore. People are beginning to realize how contemporary life, which is much more materially comfortable, is arguably socially and spiritually more severe than for the technologically challenged Yahi. Some are gaining awareness that, as medicine man Sun Bear, of the Chippewa tribe, said, ". . . the measure of a civilization . . . should not be in the height of its concrete buildings, but rather how well its people have learned to relate to their environment and fellow man."[4]

These conditions are causing a growing sense that society is sliding toward spiritual and social bankruptcy. Increasingly, society can be seen as a great heartless machine rolling over the social and spiritual practices of people. If the silent majority had a collective voice, it might say, "I have lost my way, and I don't know how to find my way back to wholeness. I am lonely and sad, and I long for balance and harmony. I need to belong to something more fulfilling so I have more hope, but I don't know how I got here or how to find a means of escape." Such sentiments reflect the unhappiness of millions of people in society who have little sense of purpose, do not feel like they belong, are lacking connection to their spiritual dimension, and have a profound absence of the sacred without knowing why they feel a deepening sense of incompleteness.

To many people, it is clear that we have created a culture that is blindly focused on empty materialism, where scientism (the notion that real knowledge and truths can only flow from science) has effectively become the new religion trumping all other areas of human experience. In addition, it is becoming more obvious that people are being forced to serve an economic master whose morality counts for very little and whose fundamental rules are to selfishly borrow and consume at all costs, tendencies at odds with the inherent nature and requirements of the cosmos.

Questions are also emerging about an economic system that is resulting in massive inequities, where the status quo benefits the few while harming the many. We ask why, after the Great Recession of 2008, the top 25 American hedge fund managers earned over $25 billion among them (more than they made in 2007 before the crash),[5] or why three of the richest people in the world control more wealth than 600 million of its poorest inhabitants.[6] The Arab Spring and the Occupy Movement reflected the profound discontent with this system. These street protests are being joined by a growing chorus of economists predicting that the world is poised for another Great Depression.[7] People frequently ask how such economic inequities can lead to a shared interest in society that will bring stability, well-being, and peace.

It is also becoming clearer that we have developed an atomistic view of the world in which human existence is often divided into disconnected and antagonistic fragments. Instead of seeing ourselves as natural, organic, minute parts of the cosmos, as our ancestors did, we now think we are above that stature with a growing detachment from nature.

As well, we are learning that while we have largely taken man out of the village, it is much harder to take the village out of man. As we gain more scientific and technical knowledge about the natural world, we still retain our desire to belong to a tribe or community, no matter what contemporary form this takes.

We also still yearn for mystical wonder, having an innate need to connect to something greater than us. And we are becoming increasingly aware that such experiences enrich us in the midst of our fast-paced lifestyle, as expressed by Albert Einstein: "The most beautiful thing we can experience is the mysterious. It is the source of all true art and all science. He to whom this emotion is a stranger, who can no longer pause to wonder and stand rapt in awe, is as good as dead: his eyes are closed."[8]

Considering the priorities and characteristics of our current society, many people would claim that the cost we are paying for material wealth and conveniences is too high. Some would point to the 200 million Americans who say they are likely to seek help for stress or the 20 million who suffer from depression—with one in every 10 Americans taking antidepressants.[9] Others would cite widespread societal substance abuse, the high rate of divorce and family breakups, the high number of the poor incarcerated or homeless, as well as the widening gulf between rich and poor. In their book *The Spirit Level: Why More Equal Societies Almost Always Do Better,* Richard G. Wilkinson and Kate Pickett show how increasing income inequality in America is leading to increasing social and health problems as illustrated in figure 1.[10]

With hope for a better future in mind, this book examines the current economic model, assessing the status quo to understand the deeper reasons for the spiritual and social crisis sweeping Western society. It does not aim to turn back the clock or idealize bygone societies, recognizing that we unquestionably live in a better material climate. It further explores possible changes that will lead to a more balanced, socially kinder way of living. In doing so, it assesses how ancient social and spiritual knowledge of various cultures might be adapted to modern society for the benefit of all since such wisdom represents repositories of knowledge gathered and refined over time to suit the slowly evolving social and spiritual needs of the human animal. But it asserts that we need to understand how the technological, economic, and material gains from modern civilization can be blended with past wisdom from all cultures to create a better society in the future. Pursuing this inquiry, some emphasis will be placed on the Native American culture of the author. Perhaps it is finally time to begin

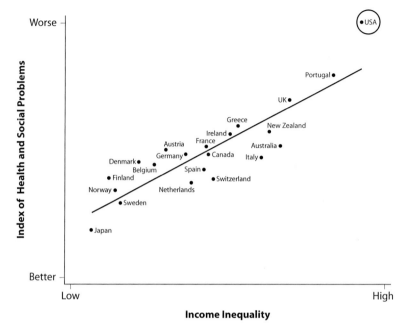

FIGURE 1 *Greater Inequality Leads to Increasing Health and Social Problems*

looking at the possibility of realizing the prophecy for the future of Oglala Sioux medicine man Crazy Horse, who said:

> Upon suffering beyond suffering: the Indigenous Nation shall rise again and it shall be a blessing for a sick world. A world filled with broken promises, selfishness and separations—a world longing for light again. I see a time of Seven Generations when all the colors of mankind will gather under the Sacred Tree of Life and the whole Earth will become one circle again . . . I salute the light within your eyes where the whole Universe dwells. For when you are at that center within you and I am that place within me, we shall be one.[11]

Part I of this book examines the structure of our current economic model and its economic, social, psychological, and spiritual impacts. Part II discusses aspects of a vision for a new economic model that better addresses our social and spiritual well-being as well as our economic needs. Finally, Part III explores how we can incorporate the knowledge of past societies into a vision for a new economic model that can lead to a more holistic well-being that includes our social and spiritual dimensions.

PART I

When Myths Make a Mess

MIDNIGHT RAIN

Lightning flash
Rolling thunder
Karma low
Life asunder.

Cumulonimbus
Darkly looms
Message pure
Self-made tomb.

Squall arising
Darkness grows
Altering course
Renewing prose.

Midnight rain
Pelting earth
Time for action
Calm the firth.

In the morn
Sunny day
Spirits show
Nobler way.

Heart reveals
Deceitful dance
Soul discloses
Hurtful trance.

Midnight rain
Plant the seed
Blossoms grow
On wisdom's feed.

Chapter 1

ECONOMIC MODEL OUT OF BALANCE

The fatal metaphor of progress, which means leaving things behind us, has utterly obscured the real idea of growth, which means leaving things inside us.

—GILBERT K. CHESTERTON

*E*very society is driven by its current myth, or mythos, a pattern of beliefs expressing the prevalent attitudes of a society. The current mythos emphasizes the separation of people from nature, the idea of "every person for themselves," and the notion that power, material possessions, and money are of paramount importance. This mythos promotes an economic model encouraging unrealistic growth, touts money as the key to well-being, and idolizes those who "win financially at all costs," such as capitalists, entrepreneurs, bankers, and hedge fund managers, while ignoring their morality and social and spiritual attitudes.

This mythos, which has shaped the cultural mind-set of the population, encourages individual greed, domination, narcissism, and consumption—all characteristics of today's society—and downplays the value of morality, spirituality, and social responsibility.

In the current situation, most people feel like they are trapped in an economic hamster wheel, expending all their time and energy chasing illusory gains, since they are governed by an economic model that requires them to use most of their effort to pay off debt with little hope for escape to a better way of life. As examined in my previous book *The Economic Dependency Trap*, this economic model promises material prosperity but blinds us to the way that the debt we incur traps us in an unsustainable cycle of stress and potential misery. Or, to use another metaphor, our current mythos is like a car, and our economic model that largely dictates how we spend our time, its engine. To survive and provide for our families, we are all pulled along by this engine while feeling we have no control over where the car goes.

FIGURE 2   *The Economic Hamster Wheel*

Since everything is connected in life, if we spend our time engaged in spiritually and socially unhealthy pursuits, our well-being will be negatively impacted. Consequently, this inquiry will begin a look at the economic model that drives our lives while having unintended harmful impacts on our well-being.

Part I provides an overview of the central features of this economic model and critically examines aspects of the prevailing cultural mindset and how it harmfully impacts the social and spiritual interests of people.

LOOKING INTO THE FISCAL ABYSS

When the white man "discovered" this country, Indians were running it.
No taxes, no debt, and women did all the work.
White man thought they could improve on a system like this?

—OLD CHEROKEE SAYING

Since the Great Recession of 2008, the world has caught a glimpse of the frightening fiscal abyss exposed by the workings of the current economic model. Most people assume that economics is a complex science practiced by those high priests of finance, economists, whose esoteric knowledge provides guidance to the masses, a flattering view that economists like to perpetuate. Take, for example, former Federal Reserve chairman and idol of economists Alan Greenspan, who was known for his disdain of regulation of the financial industry[1] and attained an almost godlike status as maestro of economists. Yet, for all of their much-touted learning and insight, neither Greenspan nor virtually any other economist predicted the economic meltdown that was the Great Recession of 2008. Greenspan later admitted in a congressional hearing that he made a mistake in presuming that financial firms could regulate themselves, and his deregulation policy is now held up as one of the leading causes of the mortgage crisis.[2]

The silver lining in the current economic cloud may be that it can function to make us more aware of our needs for the future. Philosopher Friedrich Nietzsche wrote, "When you look into the abyss, the abyss also looks into you."[3] We need to critically examine those features of the economic model that shape our cultural mind-set to assess which may no longer be beneficial for the well-being of individuals or our society. An important lesson from the Great Recession of 2008 is that economists and the economic model that they promote require critical examination for their benefits by ordinary citizens. In addition to discussing the economic model, the chapters in Part I will examine the following related fundamental pillars of the American cultural mind-set:

- unbridled consumption is good for everyone,
- the national economy can continue growing forever and must for "progress" to be sustained;
- the market is the best method of determining the efficiency of the economy and should be the predominant basis for all decisions made in society; and
- consumer debt allows for greater freedom in purchasing goods so more people can own more and better possessions and have a higher standard of living

VICIOUS CYCLE OF CONSUMPTION

I am poor and naked, but I am the chief of the nation. We do not want riches, but we do want to train our children right. Riches would do us no good. We could not take them with us to the other world . . . We want peace and love.

—CHIEF RED CLOUD (MAKHIPIYA-LUTA), SIOUX

My cousin would joke that there are "only a few shopping days left until my birthday." His jest sums up what many refer to as the worst addiction of modern America—unbridled, "soul-sucking" consumption—which has become a fundamental pillar of the American cultural mind-set.

For those on the outside looking in, the American dream is not so much about democracy and equal rights for all but about attaining an überlifestyle of having lavish material goods, comforts, and entertainment. America is seen as a consumer heaven where every meaningful event is used as an excuse to buy unneeded material possessions. Holidays in America, as well as in other countries, for example, have become less about the family celebrations and more about consumption. It is amazing how even Boxing

Day, traditionally a day of rest and socializing over drinks and food, has been turned into the mother of all shopping orgies. Shopping malls, those enticing palaces of consumption, have replaced public town squares as central places where people gather to socialize.

The contemporary mantra promoted by the powerful advertising and marketing industry is that the only route to happiness is to consume ever more stuff. In 2012, advertising spending in North America was $179.5 billion and is projected to reach $204.6 billion by 2016.[4] The pressure that such extensive advertising and marketing puts on modern families is tremendous. Parents of poor and middle-class families are knocking themselves out trying to keep their kids dressed with the latest designer jeans and fancy sneakers. Relentless marketing campaigns bombard children with messages suggesting that you are somehow inadequate or incomplete without the newest products. Purposely targeting and manipulating the insecurities of a vulnerable young population in this manner is not good for their self-esteem or their happiness. Often, parents are pressured by their children to buy the hottest-selling product so they can be "cool." Peer pressure translates directly into parental pressure and gives children an unrealistic and skewed perspective on the value of material possessions, making them feel an unwarranted sense of entitlement.

When I was a kid, I remember one Christmas morning visiting the home of a friend from an impoverished family. When my friend's ill-mannered little sister opened the modest present from her single mother and it did not meet her expectations, she said, "Is that all I get?" Her mother said nothing but responded with an expression of utter hopelessness that will forever be etched in my mind. Even billionaires do not escape the pressure to constantly purchase goods. Media sources send them the message that the only route to genuine happiness is to purchase things even more spectacular than their wealthy peers.

Such messages have supplanted the real lessons learned from millennia of social evolution prior to the consumer age about what makes people happy: having close social relations within your family, friends, and community; feeling loved, useful to, and valued by them; and having a meaningful life's purpose. With such a cultural mind-set, people define themselves and others by the material goods they own (or appear to own, in this era of huge personal debt) instead of judging individuals by the results of their actions, their intellects, skills, and characters. Frequently, the love of a family member is measured by the cost of their gifts, with purchases often becoming substitutes for affection. Enormous pressure is put upon the entire population in the race "to keep up with the Joneses." Most people have simply forgotten that life is not about what individuals own but about what kind of people they are and the type of principles by which they live.

It has been suggested that consumerism has succeeded where other ideologies have failed in America because it ". . . concretely expressed the political ideas of the century—liberty and democracy—with relatively little self-destructive behavior or personal humiliation."[5] What we are now witnessing, however, is the ultimate expression of self-destructive behavior that is no doubt contributing to much personal humiliation and suffering. Though it may have taken over a century, the chickens of unbridled consumption have come home to roost in the form of self-destructive behavior resulting in massive individual and government debt incurred as consumption is encouraged to spur growth. Thus, the very capitalist system that provides material riches has a fundamental flaw that is creating enormous personal strain. At a time when the population is drowning in debt, the prescription from governments and many economists is for people to continue spending more and incur more debt to amp up the Gross Domestic Product numbers. Arguably, consumption is also one of the greatest causes of spiritual and social disconnectedness.

Most people do not understand that the measurement known as the Gross Domestic Product, the yardstick by which nations gauge their comparative well-being, is deeply flawed because it is based primarily on consumption by the population, rather than on a broad range of aspects that reflect national well-being. Since in our current economic model,

70 percent of our national GDP[6] typically results from personal consumption as shown in figure 3,[7] *the economic well-being of America is largely determined by consumer spending by individuals.*

Typical Annual GDP

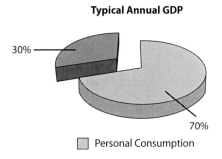

FIGURE 3 *Personal Consumption as a Share of GDP*

A consequence of the GDP being based primarily on consumer spending is the need to encourage ever more consumption. Developed nations rely heavily on emotional manipulation of their populations to consume more goods through marketing and advertising with illusory promises of prosperity.

One source indicates that from 2000 to 2007, private consumption actually accounted for an unbelievable *80 percent of U.S. GDP growth.*[8] Even more incredibly*, since 1990, the United States has accounted for one-third of the total growth in global personal consumption* while consuming approximately one-third of the world's resources.[9] Comparatively, worldwide, consumer spending now represents nearly 60 percent of global GDP.[10] Not surprisingly, such GDP growth has also led to an increase in consumer debt—a major factor in decreasing, rather than contributing to, well-being as rising GDP might falsely suggest.

Building the economic foundation of society upon consumption initially resulted in tremendous gains in standards of living—particularly in the post–World War II climate when America was largely the manufacturing hub for the world. However, now, China and other nations such as

India have replaced America in this role producing goods relatively inexpensively for massive populations aspiring to consume at the levels of Americans.[11]

The way in which this economic model has trapped Western nations into a vicious cycle of consumption and artificially created economic dependency is illustrated in figure 4. When we have debt fueling unbridled consumption, it creates a vicious cycle that harms individuals in society in ways that were not initially foreseen and are only just becoming recognized and understood.

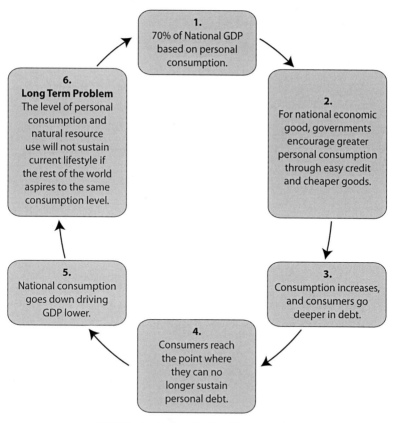

FIGURE 4 *Vicious Cycle of Consumption*

Today, it is ironic that to shore up national GDP, governments are recommending increases in personal consumption as a cure for lagging GDP when citizens are already saddled with the greatest debt loads ever. On this point, billionaire speculator George Soros aptly criticized Americans for "living in a fool's paradise" based on the false promise that debt-fueled consumption was a sustainable and legitimate economic policy.[12] An economic model based on something which people are not able to do cannot be sustained.

The inherent limitations of this economic model based on the necessity of consumption are becoming evident. If consumption is limited by finite natural resources and increasing populations, it is obvious that such a model is not sustainable. It is not possible to grow an economy based on exploiting world resources forever when those resources are limited, population is substantially increasing, and demand is escalating in rapidly developing nations. While historically it was possible for developed Western nations to entertain such a notion of continuous consumption, with huge and rapidly developing populations in China, India, Brazil, and Indonesia adopting consumption-based economies, the limits are apparent. If we consider that America has 4.5 percent of the world's population and consumes 25 percent of the world's resources, it is evident that it will be impossible for much greater populations to have the same level of material living when natural resources are already overtaxed.

As will be discussed in Part III, we need a more sustainable economic model that does not take us over the financial, spiritual, and social precipice, as well as a better way of measuring the real well-being of nations, including other things that make life worthwhile besides consumption and material possessions. To achieve these goals, we need to engage in a dialog about how we can change our consumption-based cultural mindset in the least disruptive manner. As Robert Kennedy pointed out almost 45 years ago, for "Too much and too long, we seemed to have surrendered personal excellence and community values in the mere accumulation of material things. *Our Gross Domestic Product [GDP] . . .*—if we should judge America by that—*. . . measures everything in short, except that what makes life worthwhile.*"[13] [Emphasis added]

In itself, consumption is not a bad thing. People do need to consume goods and services to survive. It is *excessive consumption* that creates problems. Chris Clugston suggests that: "*Excessive consumption does not mean that we are consuming more than we need,* which is probably also true in most cases; *it means that we are consuming at levels that are not sustainable* [personally because it creates excessive debt when uncontrolled, or globally because of limited natural resources]."[14] [Emphasis added]

Chapter 2

FALLACY OF THE GROWTH IMPERATIVE

Growth for the sake of growth is the ideology of the cancer cell.
— **EDWARD ABBEY**

*G*overnments continuously emphasize the importance of economic growth as necessary for "progress"—another fundamental pillar of the American cultural mind-set. Benjamin Franklin provided a possible rationale underlying this view, suggesting, "Without continual growth and progress, such words as improvement, achievement, and success have no meaning."[1] What politicians and economists call "consumer confidence" is simply a bellwether of optimism regarding whether people are prepared to spend money to consume more stuff to contribute to economic growth.

There is, however, a structural rationale for why growth has become imperative. To understand this, we must comprehend how the economic model creates the money supply. While many people think that a nation's money supply is created when governments print bills or mint coins, the reality is that only 2 percent is created this way. The remaining 98 percent is created when privately owned financial institutions create debt through making loans.

At the time loans are made, the only "new" money created is the principal amount borrowed. To provide the additional money supply to repay the interest on the loan, another loan has to be created. In other words, the compounding interest nature of how we create our money supply through bank loans means there is never enough money in existence to repay our loans. So, banks—not governments—create at least 98 percent of the monies in circulation and count it as their own asset "temporarily on loan to the economy" in their books through simply making computer entries.[2]

One of the most compelling warnings about such a debt-money creation system was made by Lord Josiah Wood, former director of the Bank of England, who noted, "The modern banking system manufactures money out of nothing. The process is perhaps the most astounding piece of sleight of hand that was ever invented. Banking was conceived in iniquity and born in sin. Bankers own the earth: take it away from them, but leave them with the power to create credit, and with the stroke of a pen they will create enough money to buy it back again . . . If you want to be slaves to the bankers, and pay the costs of your own slavery, let the banks continue to create money."[3]

It is not surprising, then, that distinguished economist John Kenneth Galbraith said, "The study of money, above all other fields in economics, is one in which complexity is used to disguise the truth or to evade the truth, not reveal it. *The process by which banks create money is so simple the mind is repelled.* With something so important, a deeper mystery seems only decent."[4] [Emphasis added]

Further, ordinary people also have another misconception about how banks create money. When asked how banks create debt, they often answer that they lend other depositors money. But most of modern money is just abstract, insubstantial numbers without any physical substance. Michael Rowbotham explained that the way banks create money is not by loaning preexisting money but by simply creating a computer entry as debt (a "loan") on their electronic books against the amount of money deposited with it at the time.[5] Sir Andrew Crockett, former general manager of the Bank of International Settlements, described the money creation process of banks and its weaknesses in the following way:

> Taking the banking system as a whole, the act of lending creates, as a direct consequence, deposits exactly equal to the amount of lending undertaken. Provided, therefore, banks all move forward in step, there appears to be no limit to the amount of bank money they can create. Even more than this, there would appear to be a basic instability in the banking system.[6]

David C. Korten further summarized the process of money creation in America in the following way:

> Money is created out of nothing (fiat lux) when a government prints a number on a piece of paper or a bank issues a loan and credits the amount to an account in its computers. It has no substance or inherent utility, and since President Nixon took the U.S. dollar off the gold standard in 1971, the governments and the banks that create it no longer back it with anything of any value.[7]

When this money is, in turn, paid out by bank customers to others to honor their debts, it results in more bank deposits, creating a "boomerang effect" whereby the original "loan" rapidly creates twice the amount of money supply by generating an equivalent amount of new bank deposits in the banking system.

The ability of banks to lend money beyond the amounts originally deposited or lent to them (from government-controlled banks) is called the "multiplier effect," and according to theory, at least, it should not be possible for an economy to be operated on bank-created credit. However, legal restrictions on banks such as the "liquidity ratio" (the strict limits to the amounts of money banks can create via loans) and the "reserve/asset ratio" (requirement that banks have a sufficient amount of their own money to cover loans that might default and not be repaid) have largely been abandoned. Rowbotham points out how, in the United Kingdom, the only legal requirement/asset reserve on banks is that 0.5 percent of their assets be with the Bank of England in the form of notes and coins—a totally irrelevant amount, financially speaking.[8]

The catch-22 nature of this system is clear. Governments need consumers to spend since 70 percent of the GDP depends on it. They encourage

FIGURE 5 *Impact of Banks Creating Debt*

debt-strapped consumers to spend through lowering interest rates and by eliminating restrictions on lending institutions by lowering liquidity and reserve/asset ratios to increase the multiplier effect, and, therefore, the money supply. Anyone with common sense should be able to see that this system is unsustainable in the short term—since consumers are already overleveraged—and in the long term—because finite natural resources will restrict the expansion of such an economic model.

The result of a system where economic activity depends on money, and money is almost always created by the banks as debt, is that economic activity comes to depend upon debt, which relies, in turn, on consumption. Unfortunately, such debt is now increasingly comprised of individual debt, the bulk of which is made up of home mortgages. The upshot of an economy dependent on borrowing to increase the money supply is a financial system in which both debt and money supply escalate, and the society and its individuals are punished (with debt) for the borrowing they have been forced to undertake.[9]

It is also important to realize that when banks create such "bank debt-money," the interest to pay that bank debt-money back is not created as money when the original bank loans are made. The result is that the interest can only be paid if additional interest-bearing loans are created as money. This means there is never enough money in the system to pay bank interest without creating more debt, so that this interest is essentially unpayable. This is why governments continually extoll perpetual economic growth—economies have to grow just to service existing debt.

This has two inevitable results. As total debt grows exponentially, it will eventually become unpayable once new bank debt-money creation can no longer be supported. Also, because money is extinguished as loan principals get paid off, attempts to pay off the debt set up a money shortage that triggers demand for more borrowing just to preserve the money supply.[10] In other words, the system is rigged to create a continuous money shortage and unrepayable debt.

The practical financial result of this economic model is that to pay off existing debt, governments have to incessantly tout continuous economic growth to their populations to be able to repay escalating debt. Like the needle in the arm of a drug addict, they keep telling the public that consumer spending is good for them when it is plain to those not "drinking the Kool-Aid" that it has a variety of harmful impacts. The results of economic growth created by bank-created debt-money supply is illustrated in figures 6 and 7.

Government Created Money	• Only 2 percent of printed paper currency or minted coins in the United States and Canada is created this way • Known as "fiat money" created out of nothing by decree • Low cost and no interest payments associated with making it

Bank Created Money	• 98 percent of United States and Canadian money is in the form of bank debt • Created as debt when a bank makes a loan entered in a computer as debt, and largely not from loaning pre-existing depositors money (since liquidity ratio and reserve asset ratios are being largely abandoned) • Expensive money because of interest payments associated with making it • Economy becomes dependent on debt, which is increasingly made up of consumer borrowing • Leads to unreachable cycle of debt since interest payments on such debts are not created when debt is originally created (leading to continuous scarcity of money supply) • Results in transfer of individual and national assets to banks

FIGURE 6   *Results of Bank-Created Money Supply*

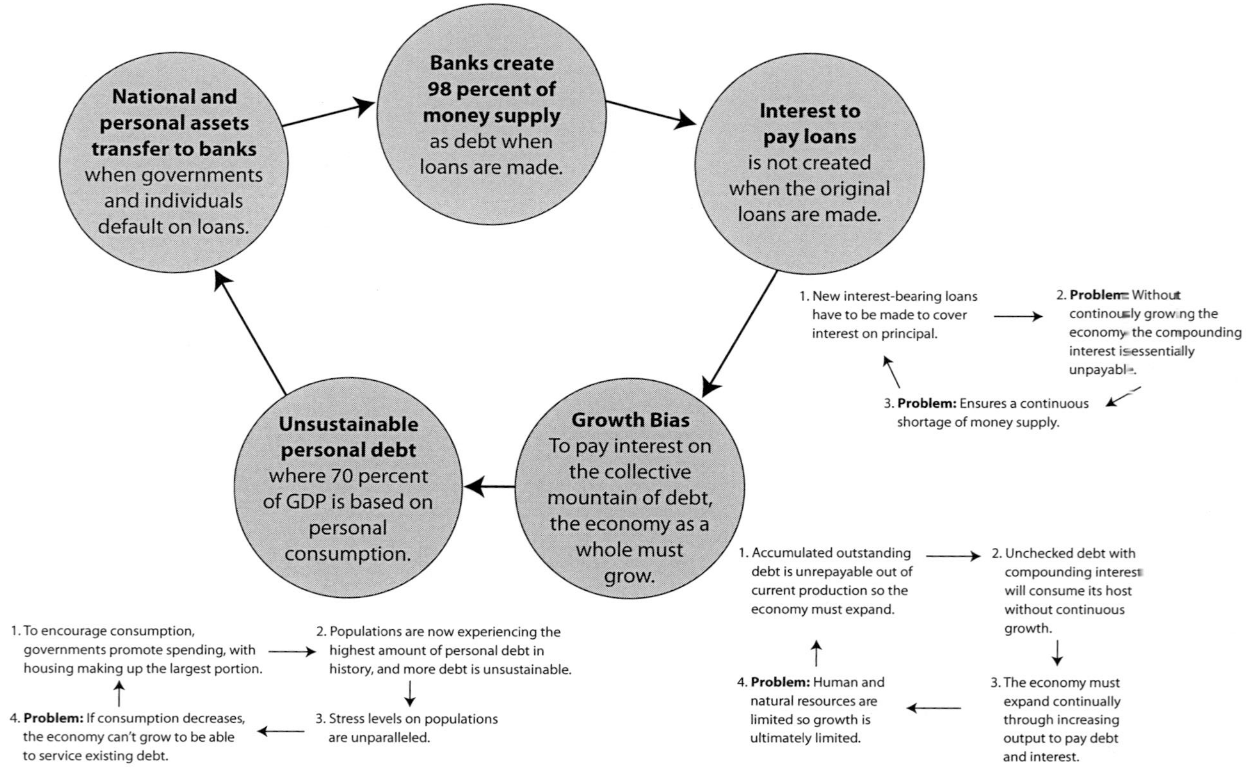

Interest to pay loans is not created when the original loans are made.

1. New interest-bearing loans have to be made to cover interest on principal.

2. **Problem:** Without continously growing the economy the compounding interest is essentially unpayable.

3. **Problem:** Ensures a continuous shortage of money supply.

Banks create 98 percent of money supply as debt when loans are made.

Growth Bias To pay interest on the collective mountain of debt, the economy as a whole must grow.

1. Accumulated outstanding debt is unrepayable out of current production so the economy must expand.

2. Unchecked debt with compounding interest will consume its host without continuous growth.

3. The economy must expand continually through increasing output to pay debt and interest.

4. **Problem:** Human and natural resources are limited so growth is ultimately limited.

National and personal assets transfer to banks when governments and individuals default on loans.

Unsustainable personal debt where 70 percent of GDP is based on personal consumption.

1. To encourage consumption, governments promote spending, with housing making up the largest portion.

2. Populations are now experiencing the highest amount of personal debt in history, and more debt is unsustainable.

3. Stress levels on populations are unparalleled.

4. **Problem:** if consumption decreases, the economy can't grow to be able to service existing debt.

FIGURE 7 *Paradox of Economic Growth Created by Bank-Created Debt-Money Supply*

Another common misconception people have about money is that we only pay interest on the money we borrow. In fact, most people would be further astounded to learn that an estimated 30 to 50 percent of interest costs are already embedded in everything that is bought and sold.[11] In other words, the real cost of the $800 iPad might actually be $400 if there were no interest charges associated with its production.

Furthermore, an inevitable consequence of funding an economy based on debt is that the assets of the country are gradually transferred to privately owned financial institutions. Thomas Jefferson issued the following warning about banks acquiring a nation's assets and leaving people in a state of dependency:

> If the American people ever allow the banks to control the issuance of their currency, first by inflation and then by deflation, the banks and the corporations that will grow up around them will deprive people of all property *until their children will wake up homeless on the continent that their fathers occupied.* The issuing power of money should be taken from the banks and restored to Congress and the people to whom it belongs. I sincerely believe that banking institutions having the issuing power of money are more dangerous to liberty than standing armies.[12] [Emphasis added]

A final misconception about the money in America is the view about who owns and controls the nation's most powerful economic institution: the Federal Reserve Bank. Most people believe that the Federal Reserve Bank is a public institution of the government.[13] The "Fed" is part public and part private. On the one hand, the Board of Governors is an agency of the U.S. government. On the other hand, it is a privately owned institution in the sense that its 12 regional member banks are privately owned bank corporations. In other words, the most powerful institution in the country (and arguably in the world), which ultimately controls the economic destiny of every citizen through its powers to determine monetary policy, interest rates, the issuance of money, the control of reserve requirements for private bank loans, is, according to Anthony Sutton, professor of economics, California State University, Los Angeles, a ". . . legal private monopoly of the money supply operated for the benefit of a few under the guise of protecting and promoting public interest."[14]

In summary, the flaws of the current debt-based money creation system are the following: The accumulating interest on debt is unpayable. The debt is increasing exponentially. There is a growing shortage of money relative to debt. The system is inherently unstable because it attempts to defy mathematical law. Finally, it is subject to the whim of the Federal Reserve Bank, a largely privately owned institution, whose decisions to increase or decrease the money supply are made in secret.[15]

If this were not the way our financial system actually operated, most people would believe it was a looney form of hucksterism or a kind of government-sanctioned Ponzi scheme. It has numerous negative impacts. First, the economic hamster wheel effect forces people to put increasing time and energy into trying to keep up financially, putting populations under ever-increasing stress. Second, the GDP measurement which governments use to measure the nation's well-being does not reflect the whole picture and is actually a misleading indicator of well-being that obscures people's more wide-ranging needs. Third, the notion that economies can grow forever is unrealistic in the real world of limited natural resources where development is exacting a huge ecological and environmental toll on a planet that is getting smaller with massive increases in population. Fourth, it falsely promotes unbridled consumption, leading to debt slavery.

All these impacts have undermined the well-being of people in society because as governments acquire more debt, they need more personal consumption and essentially seek to grow the economy on the backs of an already debt-fatigued population. Consequently, the debt pressure that governments feel is forced onto an already overstressed population with alarming social and spiritual consequences.

However, the unrealistic fantasy of governments and economists, that perpetual economic growth is necessary and possible, may be coming to

SURPRISING FACTS ABOUT MONEY AND THE ECONOMIC MODEL

Myth—All money is created and printed by government-controlled banks or treasury.

Fact—In the United States and Canada, only about 2 percent of the money supply is in the form of currency or minted coins, and 98 percent is in the form of loans or debt created by private banks when they issue mortgages, student, or business loans, or when the government issues a government debt bond.

Result—Citizens and governments are left out of the potentially significant benefit of printing currency or minting coins at a minuscule cost to taxpayers and, instead, collectively pay interest on all that we buy and sell on massive growing debts initially created by private banking corporations (which are held widely by individuals and businesses).

Myth—Our standard of living is keeping pace with our debts.

Fact—In the United States, between 1950 and 2005, total outstanding debt (household, business, government, and foreign) has increased 86 times compared with 40 times for the GDP.

Result—Debt load is dramatically outstripping economic growth.

Myth—With proper measures, like a personal mortgage, we will still be able to pay the total outstanding debt of nations.

Fact—The total outstanding debt of nations is unrepayable out of the current and future production of our households and businesses—in other words, entire nations and the world itself are mortgaged.

Result—A growing mountain of debt forces society into an endless, and, ultimately, unstoppable loop of economic growth where new money must be constantly lent.

Myth—Currency speculation is no big deal.

Fact—An estimated $2 trillion in currencies per day are traded around the world (approximately 90 percent of this is accounted for by speculation that is unrelated to the sale of goods and services), or, in other words, $730 trillion per year is created through currency speculation.

Result—The global annual casino economy of currency speculation amounts to 12 times more than the world's total income or Gross World Product of $65 trillion (2006).

Myth—In the United States, the central bank, the most powerful institution in the country, known as the "Fed," is a public institution owned by the government.

Fact—The Federal Reserve Bank is a part government and part privately owned institution. The private part consists of 12 regional banks owned and controlled by its member banks, which themselves are privately owned bank corporations. It is criticized for being created as a cartel to protect its banking members from competition by seven wealthy Americans (who represented, at the time, one-fourth of the entire wealth of the world).

Result—The Federal Reserve, the most powerful institution in the country that controls monetary policy, interest rates, the issuance of money, the control of reserve requirements for private bank loans, and, ultimately, the economic destiny of every citizen, is largely a legal private monopoly of the money supply operated for the benefit of a few under the guise of promoting public interest.[16]

(**Source:** Mark Anielski, *The Economics of Happiness*[16])

an end sooner than we think. According to author Richard Heinberg in his book *The End of Growth,* the three primary factors barring such future economic growth are:

(1) important natural resource depletion—especially fossil fuels and minerals;

(2) negative environmental impacts from the extraction and use of resources; and

(3) financial disruptions arising from the existing inability of the monetary, banking, and investment systems to adjust to:

    a. the scarcity of natural resources;

    b. soaring environmental costs; and

    c. their inability in a shrinking economy to service enormous amounts of public and private debt.[17]

In addition, there are also other factors that may put a damper on the growth imperative in the future. One factor is that the original justifications for consuming, such as stimulating employment and economic activity with American-made goods, no longer apply as much since more goods are manufactured cheaply overseas and their production is not employing the people buying them. Unlike 1929, at the end of President Coolidge's presidency, when the United States was producing 42 percent of the world's manufactured goods,[18] or after World War II when it was producing 60 percent of the world's manufacturing output,[19] in 2007, it had a trade deficit in manufactured goods of $499 billion.[20] In the same year, the U.S. trade deficit with China shot up 10 percent, to $256 billion, and with Mexico, it soared 16 percent to $73 billion—record trade deficits with these countries.[21] Figure 8 illustrates the impact on the American GDP of manufacturing abroad when American consumers are overburdened with debt.

Another factor weighing against the continued growth of a consumption-based economy is changing demographics. The postwar

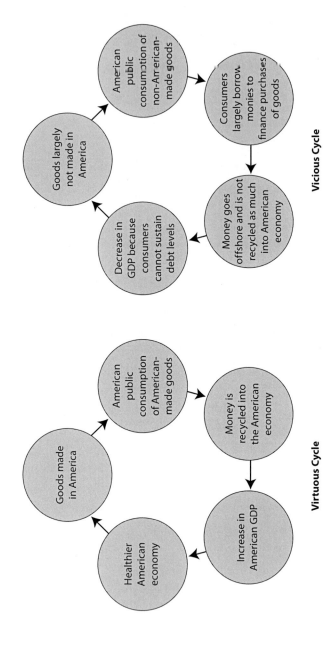

Virtuous Cycle

Vicious Cycle

FIGURE 8   *Virtuous Versus Vicious Cycle Impact from Americans Consuming Manufactured Goods Made Abroad*

baby boom population that was engaged in manufacturing production is now giving way to a more service-oriented economy where one-third of the population is getting set to retire. In the United States, there are approximately 80 million baby boomers preparing to retire, which has enormous financial implications.[22]

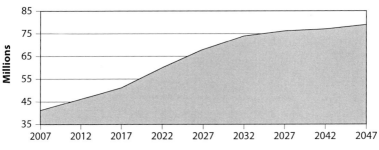

Number of Retirees by 2050

FIGURE 9 *Coming Demographic Tidal Wave*

In 1950, there were 16 U.S. workers for every retiree: by 2032, there will be only 2.1 paying for each beneficiary as illustrated in figure 10.[23]

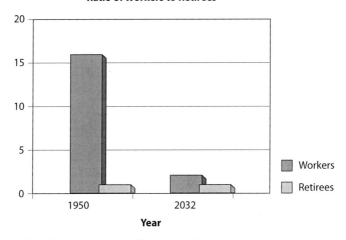

Ratio of Workers to Retirees

FIGURE 10 *Impact of Demographics on the Pension System*

By 2041, experts suggest that the U.S. pension system will be exhausted. The prospect of losing their pension weighs on the minds of America's elders.

The economic climate and demographics combine to make it increasingly difficult to return to such a consumption-reliant economy (even if this were a good thing) because the diminishing workforce that initially sustained such manufacturing is shifting available workers into a service-based economy.

The major longer-term issue regarding the growth imperative is, however, the fact that America's consumption of 25 percent of the world's resources while making up only 4.5 percent of the world's population is not sustainable for the budgets of individual consumers or the finite resources of the world. Even with declining fertility rates, United Nations population high growth projections suggest that by 2050, there could be 10.6 billion people on the planet (3.6 billion more than today), and by 2300, the population could be 36.4 billion.[24] The UN warned recently that if birth rates in developing countries continue to grow, the world's population could reach 15 billion by 2100.[25]

Unfortunately, unbridled consumption has now also become the dream for the burgeoning Chinese and Indian populations. Lester Brown, author of *Plan B 2.0: Rescuing a Planet under Stress and a Civilization in Trouble*, points out that the world simply "cannot sustain the American way of life for China's population of 1.3 billion people alone—much less for China, America and India together . . . [a combined population approaching 3.3 billion]."[26] At the current pace, Brown points out, before midcentury, China will be consuming more oil and paper than the world now produces.[27] He notes further that "the western economic model—the fossil-fuel based, auto-centered, throwaway economy—is not going to work for China."[28]

The impact of the Chinese, with over three times the population of the United States, on natural resource consumption, is just beginning to be felt. In fact, in 2009, it was reported that China surpassed America as the world's largest consumer of energy by about 4 percent[29]—trending toward massive increases in consumption of all natural resources. However, data reveals that in the same year, the personal consumption of Chinese was only $1.6 trillion, while America consumed over $10 trillion in personal goods.[30] Figure 11 reveals that the household consumption of Americans was more than double that of the Chinese in 2008.[31] However, by 2015, China's private consumption share of GDP is projected to jump to 45 percent,[32] and by 2040, to over 60 percent.[33]

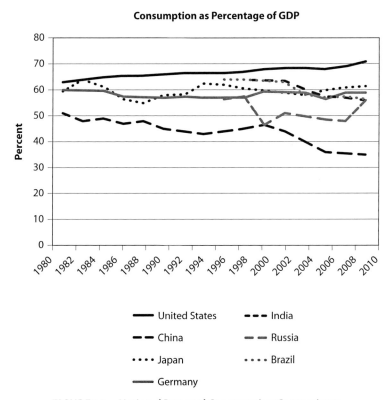

FIGURE 11 *National Personal Consumption Comparisons Among Different Countries*

In facing the unsustainability of growth, the goal should not be to stop winning economically. Instead, it should be to win wiser so as to minimize human casualties in the campaign to give people what they actually need for their well-being in a way that leads to more balance and sustainability and demonstrates greater kindness and compassion for people and respect for the environment. It should be clear that the sun is starting to set on a system that bases its economic health so much on personal consumption and materialism.

To lead the way again, we need to look at a sustainability-oriented society focused more on the wise use of finite resources—not just a greener economy but a smarter one.

Chapter 3

GETTING CAUGHT IN OUR OWN MOUSETRAP

Man is the only kind of varmint that sets his own trap, baits it, then steps in it.

—JOHN STEINBECK

*T*here are several ways in which the current mythos of our society and its resulting economic model have affected individuals in harmful ways beyond causing financial problems. This chapter explores some of the more significant social and personal impacts.

WHEN DEBT LEADS TO SLAVERY

The pillar of the American mind-set that consumer debt allows for greater freedom in purchasing goods so people can own more and better possessions and, thus, have a higher standard of living has led to record personal and family debt resulting in debt slavery. This is causing not only economic problems but personal and social problems, such as stress leading to illness and a sense of hopelessness resulting in social isolation.

According to the National Debt Clock, today, total personal debt per American citizen is $184,459, total debt per family is $732,661, and personal debt is approximately $16 trillion.[1] Michael Rowbotham, in *Grip of Death*, underscores this idea, that our economic model is fundamentally defective since it binds us to a modern form of economic slavery so we feel trapped by debt in jobs that pay fixed wages, have insufficient purchasing power, have a fear of unemployment, and become workaholics, resulting in a lack of leisure time that should provide a healthy counterbalance to a fast-paced modern life.[2]

Similarly, blogger Ashvin Pandurangi also points out how debt has enslaved us in a way that resembles the earlier enslavement of African Americans in America:

> . . . we have millions of people up to their eyeballs in housing and consumer debts, paying upwards of 20% interest on their credit cards and "payday loans" . . . an entrenched system that forces people to work longer hours for fewer benefits and wages over time . . . where the era of global indebtedness today has come to resemble that of the pre–Civil War enslavement of African-Americans, except at a much larger scale. Is it really so unimaginable that an average lower- or middle-class American family . . . could find themselves in literal contracts of debt peonage [where laborers are bound in servitude because of debt], despite the technical "illegality" of such contracts at this time?[3]

FIGURE 12 *An Economic Model Leading to Debt Slavery*

Michael Rowbotham, in *The Grip of Death*, points out how economists as professionals are failing to deliver a model with a sustainable future,[4] and suggests that modern economic theory completely fails to take into account the insidious side effects of debt.[5]

As he further explains, government relies upon the majority of consumers going into debt because of the inherent structural defect in our economic model that requires permanent debt for the creation and circulation of money so an adequate money supply is maintained.[6] In the United States, between 1950 and 2005, the total (government, business, and household) outstanding debt increased 86 times, while GDP (economic growth) has only grown comparatively by 40 times in the same period as illustrated in figure 13.[7]

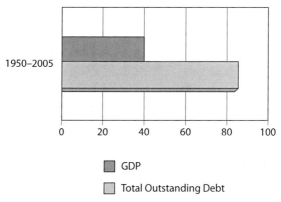

FIGURE 13   *Total Outstanding Debt Outstrips GDP*

Having trapped ourselves by debt that is an integral part of our economic model, we must now find a way to liberate ourselves from debt slavery by changing aspects of our economic model and by learning to cut back on unbridled consumption and do more with less. We need to encourage economic behavior that not only delivers smaller golden eggs but that does not kill the goose. This means altering our materialistic lifestyle and creating a new understanding of what wealth really is—one encompassing what makes people happy, rather than what they can consume that purportedly makes them happy.

WHEN STRESS LEADS TO DISTRESS

Tension is who you think you should be. Relaxation is who you are.

—CHINESE PROVERB

One indicator of the increasing pressures of modern life in America resulting from the economic model is the high level of stress which occurs when forces from the outside world impinge on individuals. In response to stress, the body releases powerful neurochemicals and hormones that prepare us for action (fight or flight), and if no action is taken, the response can lead to serious health problems. This can be especially damaging if the stress is prolonged, uninterrupted, unexpected, and unmanageable. Stress is also often cited as one of the primary reasons for the record level of obesity, which, in turn, leads to diabetes, heart disease, and other health problems.

Statistics from the American Psychological Association[8] suggest that *two-thirds* of Americans (200 million people) say they are likely to seek help for stress.[9] Stress is not only taking a physical and psychological toll on individuals, but is also deeply impacting the emotional and physical well-being of families.[10]

In a recent study, people identified the most frequent sources of stress as money (76 percent), work (70 percent), and the economy (65 percent), as illustrated in figure 14.[11] With the declining economy, a further survey by the American Psychological Association found that eight out of 10 Americans say the economy is a significant source of stress, with increasing numbers of people worrying about their finances and whether they can even provide for their family's basic needs.[12] Such stress is also being transmitted directly to children, who worry about their parents' stress levels,[13] while the parents underestimate the stress levels of their children.[14]

Another sign of a population under too much stress is the number of people becoming addicted to various legal and illegal substances, straining

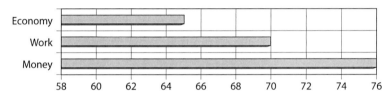

FIGURE 14 *Impact of Economic Forces on People*

the healthcare system and contributing to the illness and death of millions of Americans.[15] Despite the "War on (illegal) Drugs," currently, 20 percent of Americans risk prescription drug addiction to painkillers, stimulants, or sedatives.[16] Misuse of legal medications has become a national epidemic killing more citizens annually than die in car crashes.[17] Astonishingly, Americans now consume 80 percent of the world's opioid (opiumlike) pain medication and 99 percent of the world's hydrocodone (semisynthetic opioids).[18] As these statistics show, the recreational misuse of such narcotic drugs intended for prescription by medical doctors as pain relievers, such as morphine and oxycontin, is literally off the charts.

A further survey has revealed that over 5 million Americans are in denial over their drug abuse and require, but do not receive, treatment.[19] In turn, such substance abuse often translates into family violence, mistreatment of children, less-productive and more dangerous workplaces, and debilitating addiction and physical dependency.

Clearly, it would benefit people and add to their general well-being if the economic model could be changed to allow for more leisure time and less pressure to diminish stress in people's lives.

WHEN THE RICH HOLD THE REINS

If a free society cannot help the many who are poor,
it cannot save the few who are rich.

—JOHN F. KENNEDY

Another way our economic model has had a social and personal impact is in the growing gulf between the rich and poor that has led to an increase of various social problems. If the greatness of a society can be measured according to Winston Churchill's view—". . . by how it treats it weakest members,"[20]—America's greatness is in question. Approximately 49.1 million Americans, or 16 percent, live below the official poverty line.[21] Millions more struggle each month to pay for basic necessities or run out of savings when they lose their jobs or face health emergencies.

In 2010, the richest 20 percent of Americans held almost 50 percent of the nation's income, while 16 percent of the poorest held only 3.4 percent, as illustrated in figure 15.[22]

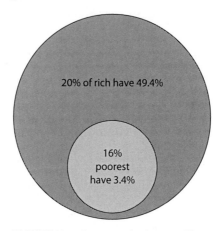

20% of rich have 49.4%

16% poorest have 3.4%

FIGURE 15 *Comparative Income Share*

As well, between 1993 and 2008, the top 1 percent of families had 52 percent of total income gains.[23] This trend has resulted in the poor and middle class feeling as if they are being squeezed out of existence.[24] Widespread awareness of such gross inequities has led to the Occupy Movement and other worldwide mass unrest.

Such poverty has also led to a greater incarceration rate among the poor. The United States has 4.5 percent of the world's population and 25 percent of the world's incarcerated population—and thus is the number-one country in the world for locking up its citizens.[25] In the time of Alexis de Tocqueville, Europeans used to come to America to study its progressive prison and penal system, but they now view it with horror.[26] According to recently released data from the federal Bureau of Justice Statistics, the number of Americans currently behind bars has reached more than 2.3 million.[27] Figure 16 compares the total country and prison populations between America, China, Russia, and 26 European countries with the largest inmate populations.[28]

Total Population (billions)

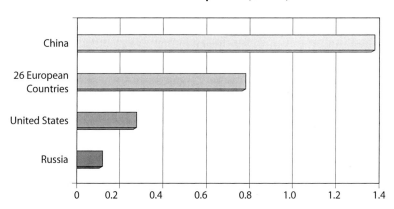

Prison Population (millions)

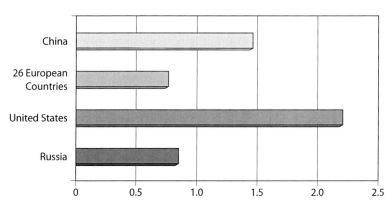

FIGURE 16   *U.S. Incarceration Rates Compared to Other Major Nations*

For poor, largely ethnic people, these statistics mean that the chances of being sent to prison are much higher than for white people.

A further social impact of the inequities between rich and poor in America is the increasing number of homeless people who are not currently getting assistance. At any given time, between five and six hundred thousand people in America are considered "homeless" without a "permanent, safe, decent, affordable place to live." Families constitute about one-third of all homeless and are the fastest-growing segment. The elderly homeless are also expected to grow rapidly as America ages.

To address these inequities and solve these social problems, we must evaluate how our economic model is impacting society and work to change it.

WHEN MARKET MAGIC LEADS TO MADNESS

I think there's a lot of merit in an international economy and global markets, but they're not sufficient because markets don't look after social needs. Markets are designed to allow individuals to look after their private needs and to pursue profit.[29]

—GEORGE SOROS

Society has evolved from a marketplace to a market economy and has now become a market society. In this new model, the logic of buying and selling is no longer just applied to material goods but increasingly governs the totality of life. Writer and philosopher Michael J. Sandel points out the difference between the two: *a market economy is a valuable and effective tool for organizing productive activity, whereas a market society is a way of life in which market values seep into every aspect of human endeavor.*[30]

There are hidden costs to a society in which market values influence every aspect of life. Sandel suggests that we should worry about such a society because of the inequality which can result and the corruption it may create.[31] In such a climate, the 600 million poorest people on the planet might ask how fair it is that the world's three richest people control so much more wealth than they do and wonder how this can make people feel they are part of a shared society. Further, there is no question that the Occupy Movement has at its roots the inequities of this current system. Politicians should be wary of a potential explosion of a middle class that is reaching its limits, a situation that has already resulted in widespread protests and violence in European countries that are undergoing tough austerity measures.

Sandel further argues that considering everything in society in terms of market value can corrupt because markets don't just allocate goods but express and promote certain attitudes toward them:

> Paying kids to read books might get them to read more, but might also teach them to regard reading as a chore rather than a source of intrinsic satisfaction. Hiring foreign mercenaries to fight our wars might spare the lives of our citizens, but also might corrupt the meaning of citizenship.[32]

A further problem with a market society is pointed out by George Soros—the fact that markets do not look after social needs but are intended to facilitate commerce by enabling the easy exchange of material goods.

When we live in a market society, we make over our social and spiritual relations in the image of the market, allowing morality, social issues, and spiritual questions to be influenced by market values. The Great Recession of 2008 provided a good example of how we can harm ourselves by allowing market values to impact these areas of life. There are good reasons why we should not permit market values to influence these aspects. Certainly one major reason is that we cannot truly raise our children right when we teach them that everything should be considered in the context of financial profits or losses, and that material possessions lead to power and happiness. Instead, we should educate our children to be happy with what they have so that they will know the true value of things.

To solve these social and personal problems resulting from our current mythos and economic model, we need to more clearly alter that model so it encompasses our social and spiritual aspects in addition to our financial concerns.

Chapter 4

THE GROWTH IMPERATIVE
AND THE ENVIRONMENT

When all the trees have been cut down,
when all the animals have been hunted,
when all the waters are polluted,
when all the air is unsafe to breathe,
only then will you discover you cannot eat money.

—CREE PROPHECY

$\mathcal{T}$he current mythos promotes a cultural mind-set that is cavalier toward the environment and other planetary life. Where populations have come to expect rising standards of living, impacts on biodiversity and the environment are inevitable. When it is clear that such an approach is not sustainable, though, it makes sense to heed the recent warning from the United Nations that humanity "must do more with less."[1] Reinforcing this point, a recent study suggests that by 2050 there will not be enough resources or space to raise livestock to produce meat and dairy products, concluding that even if the world switched to a primarily plant-based diet, there still might not be enough food to avert a catastrophic food shortage.[2]

Along the same lines, a recent OECD (an economic agency of major industrialized nations) report warned that current pressures on the earth's ecosystem are now so great that future generations are doomed to falling living standards.[3] From 1900 to the present, total annual global resource use has increased from 6 billion tons to approximately 60 billion. By mid-century, people will use 140 billion tons of four key resources—three times the current consumption.[4] We dump wastes into oceans and rivers, pollute lands, and pump harmful emissions into the atmosphere. A recent study by the World Bank revealed that in China alone, the current annual death toll from pollution is three-quarters of a million people—twice previous estimates.[5] All these problems are exacerbated by an economic model emphasizing continuous growth and maximum consumption. This chapter will examine the ways in which the mythos drives human activity to harmfully impact the environment and its biodiversity.

Total Global Annual Natural Resource Use (billions of tons)

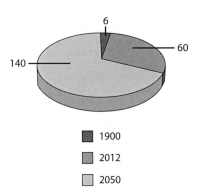

- 1900
- 2012
- 2050

FIGURE 17   *Increase of Natural Resource Use by Year*

TAKING TOO MUCH

Frugality is one of the most beautiful and joyful words in the English language, and yet one that we are culturally cut off from understanding and enjoying. The consumption society has made us feel that happiness lies in having things, and has failed to teach us the happiness of not having things.

—ELISE BOULDING

The impact of modern civilization on the environment shows the frightening stress that human activity is placing on nature. In addition, biodiversity has and continues to be lost at an unprecedented rate. It was only around three hundred years ago that Europeans looked upon the forests of North America as an infinite source of wood for industrial and military purposes. Today, industrial logging has decimated these ancient forests, leading one writer to comment, "If one were to encapsulate the entire history of Western logging into a thirty second film, its effect on the Northern Hemisphere would be comparable to the eruption of Mount Saint Helens on the surrounding forest: both represent irresistible waves of energy that originated in a relatively small, specific area and expanded rapidly, leveling everything in their path."[6]

Indigenous North Americans were similarly impacted by the demise of the great buffalo herds as hills of buffalo skeletons lined the prairies. By some estimates, it only took 10 years—from 1874 to 1884—to slaughter most of them.[7] Although no one will ever know exactly how many buffalo existed, estimates range from 25 to 70 million[8]—so many that early explorers around the time of Columbus's arrival noted that "the plains were black and appeared as if in motion" with buffalo.[9] Because indigenous North Americans used the animal for millennia, the buffalo were inextricably woven into the fabric of their daily life and their loss had a profound impact.

It appears that the human race has still not learned its lesson. The World Conservation Union[10] recently completed what has been billed as the world's most authoritative assessment of Earth's plants and animals, concluding that 16,306 of the 41,415 species are at risk of extinction.[11] A further UN report noted that current human activities are inadvertently wiping out three animal species a day.[12] According to another source, every 20 minutes, we lose an animal species and, if this pace continues, by the end of the century, 50 percent of all living species will be gone.[13]

Recently, the Yangtze River dolphin (known in China as the *baiji* dolphin) went from being one of the most endangered species on the planet to being declared officially extinct, following an intensive survey of its habitat.[14] Apparently, this is the first large vertebrate forced to extinction by human activity in 50 years and only the fourth time an entire evolutionary line of mammals has vanished from the face of the earth since the year 1500.[15]

Such developments strike close to home in my own traditional tribal territory on the northwest coast of British Columbia. There, logging is currently threatening the survival of a rare species of bear known as the Kermode bear (*Ursus americanus kermodei*) known as *mooksgm'ol* in the Sma'algyax language of the Tsimshian people. These bears represent a rare black-and-white subspecies found only in this area,[16] but it is the white Kermode, or "spirit bear," that has captured public attention. For them to survive, a large population of black bears must remain stable to sustain the gene that produces the white bear. The precarious plight of the bear has been brought to international attention by the passion and dedication of the founder of the Spirit Bear Youth Coalition, Simon Jackson,[17] who is

Saving Our Spirit Brothers
(Simon Jackson, Spirit Bear Youth Coalition Founder)

working diligently to ensure the habitat of the spirit bear is protected. If the habitat of the bear is not protected, *mooksgm'ol* will very likely remain only an animal of ancient Tsimshian legend—a special gift from Raven, the Creator, hopefully one not lost by a civilization that, it turns out, is "very clever . . . but not very wise."

The human impact on the earth has been so evident that a group of distinguished British geologists have proposed human activity, not natural processes, has pushed the planet into a new geological era[18]—leaving the Holocene and entering the Anthropocene (the Age of Man) era.[19] They contend that the environmental footprint on the earth's surface through carbon pollution, nuclear fallout, and other technology "should be recognized . . . as a 'formal epoch'."[20] This is based partially on the fact that the CO_2 in the atmosphere has increased markedly from the 300 parts per million (ppm) in 1900 to 390 ppm presently—well beyond the 278 ppm that helped stabilize climate during the lengthy Holocene period.[21]

The phenomenon of global warming is caused largely by the amount of heat-trapping CO_2 in the atmosphere. In 2011, CO_2 reached a record level of 390.0 ppm, increasing by over 40 percent since 1750 (before people began burning fossil fuels in earnest),[22] and by 2013 surpassed the threshold of 400 parts per million for the first time since measurements began, breaching a threshold not seen for 3 million years.[23] Other international research sources have found that extreme heat caused by climate change could cause an additional 150,000 deaths this century in larger U.S. cities if no immediate steps are taken to curb carbon emissions.[24] Such warming has caused the Arctic ice cap to shrink by an area twice the size of France's land mass in 2 years,[25] and in 2012, it was clear that the Arctic was warming twice as rapidly as the rest of the planet.[26] As well, 2012 was on track to become one of the top 10 hottest years on record.[27]

Another consequence of global warming is that much CO_2 ends up dissolving into the world's oceans, where it is turning the waters acidic at an unprecedented rate—much faster than at any time in the past 300 million years.[28] New sophisticated ocean acidification research reveals that climate change is making oceans more corrosive, causing dropping alkaline levels from a typical ocean pH of 8.1 to an astonishing low pH of 7.7 in Puget Sound, where the city of Seattle is located.[29] It is not necessary to be a rocket scientist to realize that global warming can massively impact the ocean food chain upon which human survival depends.[30]

Even if it turned out, against the weight of scientific evidence and the preponderance of expert opinion, that human production of CO_2 was not the cause of global warming, simple prudence and the instinct for self-preservation should dictate a more conservative approach to our activities. There may well be a tipping point in the global warming process beyond which there is a point of no return. The human race, like a heavy smoker with a bad cough, should not be willfully blind to the fact that its behavior is inflicting self-harm.

ADDRESSING NEED WITHOUT GREED

There is sufficiency in the world for man's need but not for man's greed.

—MOHANDAS K. GANDHI

In a finite world with the planet's resources already under enormous pressure, Western countries must rethink the economic model that is built on the idea that it is possible to sustain growth forever. We need to look at ways of decoupling improvements in lifestyle from the consumption of natural resources. If emerging economies want sustainability, they will have to manage their growth differently from the way industrialized nations have relied on natural resources.

We must also be mindful that in the history of the planet there already have been five major extinctions.[31] According to renowned paleoanthropologist Dr. Richard Leakey, the sixth extinction will be man-made and is already well underway with its impact on biodiversity and the environment caused by how carelessly we extract our sustenance out of nature.[32] Society needs desperately to engage in a dialog about a new mythos that might lead to a cultural mind-set more likely to sustain human existence on this small planet.

Chapter 5

WHEN THE MORAL BANK
NEEDS A DEPOSIT

*Every young man would do well to remember that all
successful business stands on the foundation of morality.*

—HENRY WARD BEECHER

As the result of writing *An Inquiry into the Nature of and Causes of Wealth of Nations* (1776), Scottish economist Adam Smith is widely regarded as the father of free-market capitalism.[1] He contended that it is human nature to be self-interested, stating, "It is not from the benevolence of the butcher, the brewer, or the baker that we expect our dinner, but from their regard to their own interest. We address ourselves, not to their humanity but to their self-love, and never talk to them of our own necessities but of their advantages."[2] It sounds as though he is saying that people are naturally selfish and, by extension, that greed is good. But, what many people overlook is that Adam Smith was also a social philosopher who taught moral philosophy at the University of Glasgow. Earlier in 1759, he published *The Theory of Moral Sentiments*, in which he defined self-interest not as selfishness or greed but as a psychological need to win favor in one's society.[3] This encompasses the notion that human morality depends on sympathy between society's members. Though human beings tend to be self-interested, they also benefit from cooperative interaction with others to secure their individual and collective well-being. In other words, if we hope to enrich ourselves economically, socially, and morally, we must constantly be aware that we are rooted in communities and that our actions and the actions of others mutually impact each other.[4] The virtue of free market capitalism should be that people can only make themselves better off by helping others.[5]

Unfortunately, recent economic turmoil in the United States has underscored the lack of morality at the highest level. In 2012, an outgoing executive of Goldman Sachs, Greg Smith, who headed the bank's European Equity Derivatives Division, wrote a scathing resignation letter published in the *New York Times* in which he claimed that the Wall Street firm was a "toxic" place, where it was common for senior executives to "talk about ripping their clients off."[6]

In the United Kingdom, greed and immorality also flourish, as indicated by the recent resignations of three top executives of Barclays Bank amid revelations that the bank "systematically" attempted to rig the London-offered Libor rates for profit.[7] The bank was fined $453 million for this "infraction" while regulators are investigating dozens of other banks around the world.[8] The Swiss bank UBS AG also recently agreed to pay a fine of $1.5 billion to settle a similar charge of interest rate rigging. Many argued that much more punishment was due since more senior people knew about and participated in the illegal activities.[9] Republican Senator Charles Grassley of Iowa, a member of the U.S. Senate Finance Committee, commented, "The reluctance of U.S. prosecutors to file criminal charges over big-time bank fraud is frustrating and hard to understand . . . [the $1.5 billion fine is a] spit in the ocean compared to the money lost by borrowers at every level, including taxpayers."[10] This affair has raised new questions about the independence of some global banking regulators, with some calling for the resignation of former longtime UBS official Mark Branson, who is now Switzerland's top banking supervisor.[11]

Further, after New York bank regulators accused Standard Chartered Bank of being a "rogue institution" which hid over 60,000 secret transactions linked to laundering over $250 billion for terrorist organizations such as Hezbollah and Iran's nuclear weapons program, the bank reached a $340 million civil settlement.[12] While a senior partner at the associated firm, Deloitte/Touche, committed suicide, no bank officials were found guilty of any wrongdoing.[13] The Royal Bank of Scotland is now under U.S. scrutiny over potential Iran-sanction violations.[14] Other banks that have settled similar allegations in the recent past include ING Bank NV, ABN Amro Bank, and Credit Suisse Group AG.[15]

Even the HSBC, "the world's local bank," has indulged in such corruption on a grand scale. It was caught laundering up to $9 billion in suspected Mexican drug cartel money and, according to a Senate subcommittee report, failed to properly monitor about $60 trillion from potentially criminal or terrorist sources.[16] HSBC has recently agreed to pay $1.9 billion, the biggest penalty ever imposed on a bank for money laundering, but while there have been some resignations, there have been no criminal charges.[17]

The immoral actions of other prominent actors in the current capitalist system would cause our honest grandparents to turn over in their graves in disgust. For example, the largest Ponzi scheme in history, operated by Bernie Madoff, was a fraud where approximately $65 billion was fleeced from the life savings of thousands of hardworking people. Stories of outrageous bonuses given to executives while workers are laid off abound— often where the pay for a single executive was more than the income earned by populations in entire small cities. Some notable cases are those of Léo Apotheker, who collected $25 million in severance and other benefits from Hewlett-Packard after less than a year on the job; CEO Samuel Palmisano of IBM, who became eligible for $170 million in retirement benefits just by waiting until he was past 60 to announce his retirement; and CEO Eugene Isenberg of Nabors Industries, who got $100 million in severance as he was pushed out the door.[18]

Even more disturbing was the lack of morality shown throughout the financial system before the Great Recession of 2008. The subprime mortgage crisis consisted of Wall Street types packaging up questionable mortgages they often knew were backed by worthless assets, then reselling them, resulting in staggering profits for the sellers while bringing the world economy to the brink of collapse. In 2011, Mervyn King, the governor of the Bank of England, referred to the crisis this precipitated as "the most serious . . . since the 1930s, if ever."[19] As a result, since America was the source of such worthless paper, the nation's image was tarnished and damaging to global "brand U.S.A." J.P. Morgan's $6 billion trading loss in 2012 underscores how excessive complexity and poor oversight still threaten many parts of the financial system more than 4 years after the catastrophic failure of Lehman Brothers.[20]

It will be difficult to maintain a cooperative and organized society if there continue to be ethical problems at the top of the economic system so the privileged few are able to pervert the system for their personal profit with a kind of Wild West opportunism creating hardships for ordinary people. At some point, people are bound to push back as with the Occupy Movement. If the actors in the system are not moral, there is a role for government to ensure that the collective economic health of the nation and its population are protected from the ethical excesses of such financial gunslingers.

When financial institutions can offer services key to the well-being of everyone in a community, their operation should be conditional on ongoing corporate social responsibility. Where they commit serious and harmful transgressions, they should face real consequences, such as the loss of their regional and national social and legal licenses to operate, as well as civil and criminal charges and confiscation of corporate and personal assets. It is difficult to imagine how such "white-collar crime" that can potentially impact everyone on the planet is less important than local criminal acts.

Everyone needs to keep in mind Adam Smith's basic lesson: While self-interest is in our nature, we also benefit from cooperative interaction with others. We can only find sustainable solutions to problems caused by our current economic model by working together in a healthy moral environment, recognizing that a society where there is no (or limited) trust is not a healthy environment in which to live or raise families. The mythos we embrace should reflect a morality that minimizes harm. Consequently, changes ensuring appropriate ethical behavior need to be part of a major overhaul required of the economic model.

Chapter 6

WHEN TIME IS MONEY

Time is the coin of your life. It is the only coin you have, and only you can determine how it will be spent. Be careful lest other people spend it for you.

—CARL SANDBURG

*A*n important concept for our lives that has been impacted by the current mind-set based on our economic model is the concept of time. We have been conditioned to equate time with money, to think of leisure time with loss of money and financial opportunities, rather than consider time in the larger context of our growth as social and spiritual human beings.

Further, our need to work or be constantly active to shoulder our burden of debt has led to a cultural mind-set of time poverty. This chapter explores the impact of our economic model and cultural mind-set on our concept of time and how it affects the quality of our social and spiritual lives.

TIME POVERTY

Time, like life itself, has no inherent meaning. We give our own meaning to time, as to life.

—JONATHAN LOCKWOOD HUIE

Time is a notion that we take for granted as fixed reality, overlooking the fact that we have the power to assign to it whatever meaning suits us, and that we create our own concept of time. In the modern world, we have been conditioned to think that time is passing nonstop, proceeding in one direction in a linear path. As the result of the mythos and its economic model, we have come to correlate time spent in more reflective activities with wasting it. As a result, we have developed "clock-consciousness," so we never think we have enough time and experience "time poverty." We tend to view time as relentlessly flowing or marching without cessation, as expressed by English poet Geoffrey Chaucer, who said, "Time and tide wait for no man."[1] As a result, we often have the sense that we are losing something we will never get back and that we never have enough time to do the things we need to do. This makes us anxious about being "on time" and about how we use time. As a result of always feeling like we are "on the clock" and moving closer to our expiration date, we are constantly trying to "manage" time or, like a wild child, feel it might escape our perceived control. So we experience "time pressure," which makes us feel rushed and never in control of our lives.

We feel so much time pressure that we have invented ideas like "quality time" to represent the notion of "better" time specifically spent with loved ones, with whom, due to work and activities, we don't usually spend sufficient time. To reset ourselves to a more normal state, we occasionally take a "vacation" from the stress of our everyday lives.

Such a view of time unquestionably has merit in that it allows people to trust one another, collectively perform activities necessary for the functioning of society, and express courtesy to those who have made the effort to plan their days in the expectation that events will transpire at appointed hours. But while this concept of time is our way of putting everyone on the same "time page," we have lost sight of the fact that it is something that humans have invented—simply a lens through which we have collectively agreed to see reality. Philosophers disagree over whether the concept of clock time is even real. In my opinion, clock time is simply another part of the way we have artificially made divisions in nature.

INDIAN TIME

Time is but a stream I go a-fishing in.

—HENRY DAVID THOREAU

Society has decided that clock time is the way we are going to proceed forward as a civilization, but it is not the only way. Prolific science fiction writer George Zebrowski commented, "Time is a relationship we have with the rest of the universe; or more accurately, we are one of the clocks, measuring one kind of time. Animals and aliens may measure it differently."[2] Further, seventeenth-century philosopher and poet Angelus Silesius emphasized the subjective nature of time:

> *Time is in your own making;*
> *its clock ticks in your head.*
> *The moment you stop thought*
> *time too stops dead.*[3]

Ancient cultures and traditions such as Incan, Mayan, Hopi, and other Native Americans, Babylonians, ancient Greeks, Hinduism, Buddhism, and Jainism have a different concept of time as cyclical, envisioning a "wheel of time" consisting of repeating ages that happen to every being of the universe between birth and extinction.[4]

Historically, Native Americans also have a different notion of time. The Western notion of clock time was originally wholly foreign to Native Americans. When French missionaries first introduced the mechanical clock to the Huron, they thought it was some living kind of thing, believing that it could hear and that when it struck it was speaking.[5] In Native American cultures, the idea of "Indian time" is often discussed. It means events will happen when conditions are right or appropriate or as suggested in Galatians 4:4 of the Bible, "in the fullness of time." The biblical passage suggests the need to slow down and perceive time more like "Indian time" so as to prepare our spirits for moments of grace that might be lost if we anxiously rush through the day.

In Native American culture, the uncertainty of "Indian time" is accepted with more flexibility and patience than in the dominant Western culture. At the same time, however, Native Americans and Aborigines have historically actually been punctual people and obedient to (usually) nature-based time signals that mattered to them.[6] While we can think of Western clock time as like standing on the bank of a river and watching it go by, we can see Native American time as jumping in the river of time and watching the bank go by. Or, as one source suggests, Native American time is like an ocean with everything happening on the surface and each event just a ripple.

TIME-OUT

The infinite is in the infinite of every instant.

—ZEN SAYING

In Mexican culture, the word *mañana* also indicates a flexible concept of time. While it is often interpreted to mean "tomorrow," it really means some unspecified time in the unspecified future. Mañana is really a polite way of never having to say "no" without having to say "yes." In Mexico, like in Ishi's tribe of the Yahi, answering definitively to questions when you are not sure of the answer is considered to be misleading and therefore rude.

The prevalent use of the word mañana reflects the fact that Mexican society has opted to operate within its own time frame and, though having to live to some extent by clock time, is not dominated by it. This flexible concept of time results in time for socializing and attending personal affairs—giving priority to living rather than working. When North Americans travel to Mexico, they sometimes express frustration that things don't work "on time," but once they recognize that there is no hurry, they relax and realize how wonderful it is to occasionally smell the roses. In this way, the concept of mañana is similar to "Indian time," a state in which people have the opportunity to appreciate life's sweet gifts just like they did when they were children.

As a society, people in North America may learn something from the Mexican or Native American approach to time, which can provide perspective to evaluate their priorities and encourage them to slow down sufficiently to improve the quality of their lives in ways not dependent on money. From this new perspective, they might realize the benefits of stepping back from stress-producing clock time in everyday life and seeking to purposely cultivate some unstructured time to share with family and friends.

I once knew a wise philosopher who said that "clock time is not real time" and suggested that real time was dictated by people's needs—the greater the need, the more pressing time became. We currently need relief from the stress-inducing pressure of clock time, a more flexible view of time that alleviates continuous time pressure and leads to paying more attention to social and spiritual priorities. Relaxation and leisure are not self-indulgent luxuries but opportunities to connect to social and environmental surroundings that can replenish spirituality and creativity. The pressure of clock time leaves people constantly switched on when human nature requires that we occasionally relax or play, as people did prior to the industrial and digital ages, allowing for connection to social groups or the spiritual dimension.

By contrast, feeling time pressure leads to anxiety and lack of perspective on what is important in life. Time pressure also leads to overextended work schedules and workaholism without any assurance of excelling. In fact, research reveals that just the perception of time pressure leads to poor performance.[7] While we obsess about our work schedules, we forget that work should only be a means to the end of leading a balanced and happy life.

Nearly one-third of the Canadian workforce define themselves as workaholics, say it is a "downer," derive no more satisfaction from it than nonworkaholics, and are "less content with life."[8] According to Professor Fred Grouzet from the University of Victoria, workaholic-type ambitions such as financial success, social recognition, popularity, power, and achievement in competitive fields lead to less long-term happiness and well-being than intrinsic goals such as personal growth, self-acceptance, family, authentic relationships, and helping others.[9] Further, a recent major study found that people in prosperous nations, where individuals spend much of their time working, can be deeply unhappy, whereas people in poverty-stricken nations, such as those in Latin America, are full of positivity and happiness.[10]

To adjust our sense of time and the value of activities, it may be useful to assess how we spend our time and what it brings us in terms of not only financial but social, psychological, and emotional benefits. While doing this, we should question whether there are material things or activities we could eliminate if we are prepared to change how we organize our lives to make them more fulfilling on all levels. For example, in one busy family, they made a list of everything they loved to do and everything they hated to do and compared lists.[11] After discovering their common likes and dislikes, the parents cut their overtime work, dropped some of their social engagements, and the family began participating together in activities in nature, which led to more familial harmony and well-being. There is nothing wrong and much that is right with valuing social, family, and spiritual pursuits more, or as much as, those focusing on financial gain.

Time management is really about planning and exercising control over the amount of effort spent on specific activities. In doing this, we need to remember to take a "time-out," setting aside the time to enjoy life—which is not about the destination but about the journey. Once we understand how the economic model increases the speed of the hamster wheel in which we all have to run, we might decide that exiting it and getting by with fewer material possessions is more important and beneficial.

We also need to consider how time pressures might be relieved by changing our imbalanced economic model so it does not dictate so much that "time is money."

PART II

Veils to Vision

WEEPING WILLOW WEEPS

Teardrops form
Joining, they seep.
Rivulets gather
Weeping willow weeps.

A call to the cosmos
Glaucoma of the soul.
Arrogance and ignorance
Taking a toll.

Seeing imperfect
Confusion of whole.
Ignoring intuition
Inflating role.

Understanding place
Knowledge to succeed.
Seeing true nature
Planting righteous seed.

Raindrops from heaven
Wash away the haze.
Remove the irritation
To weeping willow's gaze.

Chapter 7

FROM HOLISTIC TO THE ATOMISTIC

Humankind has not woven the web of life.
We are but one thread within it.
Whatever we do to the web, we do to ourselves.
All things are bound together.
All things connect.

—CHIEF SEATTLE

It used to be common sense that everything in nature, including humans, was interconnected. Native Americans shared a holistic view emphasizing the relationship between parts of the cosmos—as if the universe were an immense organism and we were simply a part of it. The notion is exemplified in the comments of the great Lakota medicine man Black Elk, who said, "Peace comes within the souls of men when they realize their relationship, their oneness with the universe and all its powers, and . . . that at the center of the universe dwells the Great Spirit, and that this center is really everywhere . . . including within each of us."[1] A similar idea is expressed in many other cultures. For example, Hindu monk Swami Vivekanada[2] noted that, "All differences in this world are of degree, and not of kind, because oneness is the secret of everything."[3]

By contrast, we now see the cosmos as "atomistic," that is, separated into disparate elements,[4] or characterized by or resulting from division into unconnected fragments,[5] as illustrated in figure 18 on page 61. The current mythos promotes the cultural mind-set that we are above and unconnected to nature, embracing an artificial view of reality based on reason. According to many individuals, development of this contrasting view occurred due to the increasing focus on science.

Almost one hundred years ago, Austrian philosopher Rudolf Steiner suggested that "science no longer has the habit of considering the human being as a member of the whole organism of the universe . . ."[6] He contended that this view was part of the rise of materialism and happened because modern science places no special value on the fact that we are standing within the cosmos looking upon the human being from an individual physical perspective only—almost never holistically.[7]

Similarly, Professor Jung Young Lee, in seeking to explain the source of knowledge of the *I Ching*, contrasted the modern scientific approach to that of ancient Chinese sages. He contended that scientists seek to understand the universe by examining small pieces of it through specialized scientific tools, while the early Chinese sages regarded nature as their laboratory and used their intuition to comprehend its mysteries. Professor Lee comments, "The Holy sages knew that they must be part of nature to find the principle that governs nature. *They did not take small pieces of isolated material as a means of knowing the whole. Rather, they wanted to know the whole through the study of the whole universe* . . . [becoming] part of nature to understand what nature is."[8] [Emphasis added] Elaborating further he suggests:

Because man wants to dominate nature, he does not understand it. *Moreover, modern science is interested in empirical analysis. It wants to see pieces separately and to generalize the whole from the observation of separate pieces . . . Because we want to be un-natural, we observe what is partial . . .* The sages not only observed nature but contemplated it so that nature and they were united. In this oneness the inner nature of what is natural is to be understood.[9] [Emphasis added]

Authors John Briggs, Ph.D., and F. David Peat, Ph.D., state further that we are now encountering the "dark side" of the path first tread 800 years ago when we separated ourselves from nature.[10] In seeking to eliminate uncertainty by controlling nature, we have come to think that we are masters of the animal kingdom and the environment—akin to minor gods and not simply part of a greater whole.

But it is important to once again recognize that we are inseparable from nature. Though the current fragmented analytical perspective of reality is sometimes useful, the view that we are unconnected to everything else can lead us down a dangerous path. It is inadequate for dealing with an overpopulated, interconnected world which requires a holistic perspective. Instead of seeking to control and dominate nature, we should accept the reality of our position as a minute part of the cosmos. Part III of this book discusses aspects of a vision for a new economic model that better addresses our social and spiritual well-being as well as our economic needs.

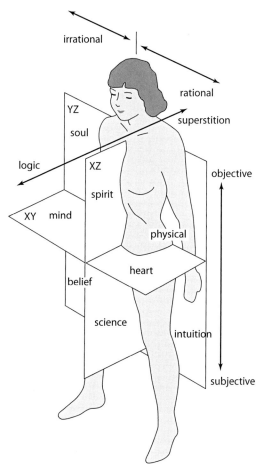

FIGURE 18 *The Atomistic Perspective on a Personal Level*

Chapter 8

THE PLACE OF PEOPLE
IN THE COSMOS

Humility is to make the right estimate of oneself.
—CHARLES HADDON SPURGEON

*A*braham Lincoln said about hubris, "What kills the skunk is the publicity it gives itself."[1] This chapter will examine how such arrogance blinds us to our real place in nature yet defines our potential.

Even though the idea that the universe was spherical with a stationary earth at its center[2] was dispelled by Nicolaus Copernicus in 1530,[3] there still is a tendency for people to think that we are not just *at* the center but *are* the center of the universe. Over three hundred years ago, French dramatist Cyrano de Bergerac complained, "The insufferable arrogance of human beings to think that Nature was made solely for their benefit, as if it were conceivable that the sun had been set afire merely to ripen men's apples and head their cabbages."[4]

Our hubris often causes us to overestimate our place in nature. But when we put our place in the cosmos in perspective, we can better appreciate our insignificance.

According to one source, the universe is at least 156 billion light-years wide[5] and is supposedly expanding all the time.[6] Comparing the estimated distance across the universe of 9.2×10^{22} miles[7] to the 7,926-mile diameter of Earth reveals its puny physical size and, by extension, our relative physical insignificance. Looked at another way, there have been estimations that there are possibly 250 billion galaxies in the universe. Within our galaxy, the Milky Way, it is thought there are 400 billion stars. If we were to assume the Milky Way is an average size for all other galaxies, that would mean that there are approximately 10^{22} solar systems in the universe—each with its own planets. If we can wrap our minds around the sheer enormity of this number, we might realize that our little planet with its conceited species Homo sapiens is barely a fleck on the flea of the cosmic elephant.

Another way of looking at our relative insignificance is in terms of galactic time. A galactic year, the time it takes for our solar system to make one revolution around the center of the galaxy, is about 226 million earth years.[8] In comparison, dinosaurs roamed the earth for about 100 million years,[9] and people are thought to have only transitioned from Homo erectus (an extinct apelike species of primitive human) to Homo sapiens a mere 300,000 to 400,000 years ago.[10] So dinosaurs survived on earth for approximately 161 galactic days, while humans have only been around for a mere 12 galactic hours.

Longevity of Homo Sapiens

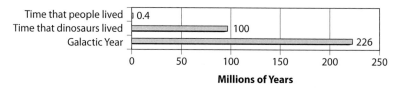

FIGURE 19   *Longevity of Homo Sapiens*

Many people have forgotten that we are simply part of nature, unwisely believing our destiny is to dominate it instead. In *Dances with Dependency*, I recounted how the Cree, as a reminder of this, reinforce the idea that individuals play a miniscule role in the larger cosmos and show true gratitude for the many daily blessings they have been granted by beginning all prayers with the following invocation: "Thank you, Creator, for giving me, such a pitiful little creature, another day and much to be thankful for."

To instill humility that inspires responsible stewardship of the environment and encourages harmonious interaction with other people, we should remember that we dwell at the bottom of the atmospheric soup of our little blue planet, having simply emerged from a much-larger whole—a cosmos of infinitely greater mystery and scale, that we are only just beginning to understand.

THE UNBEARABLE LIGHTNESS OF BEING A FLEA

We come nearest to the great when we are great in our humility.

—RABINDRANATH TAGORE, INDIAN PHILOSOPHER

It is critical to put our place in the cosmos into perspective. We need to realize that in order to maintain the attitude of humility necessary to act in the best interests of people, the environment, and the planet. We have existed for barely a nanosecond in cosmic time, and our planet is virtually immeasurable on a cosmic scale—yet, we must also comprehend the fortuitous miracle of our evolution.

With a proper attitude of humility, we may have the good fortune to choose a path that ensures survival in a manner that provides for our greatest potential happiness and fulfillment. In this spirit, one of the judgments in the Chinese classic the *I Ching*, which first appeared in 3000 BC, is *Ch'ien* (or modesty), which suggests, "Modesty brings success. The superior man who is modest can complete his works."[11] The commentary on this judgment further explains the value of humility:

> Modesty brings success. It is the way of heaven to influence the below with radiant light. It is the way of the earth, which is lowly, to go upward. It is the way of heaven to diminish the full and to increase the modest. It is the way of the earth to transform the full and to augment the modest. Spirits harm the full and bless the modest. It is the way of man to hate the full and to love the modest. Modesty that is lowly cannot be ignored. Thus the superior man will accomplish his task.[12]

To pursue a wiser, more sustainable future, we would be well served to adopt modesty, or humility, in every aspect of our daily lives as exemplified by the judgment of the *I Ching* and by the Cree prayer.

Chapter 9

RATIONING RATIONALITY
IS RATIONAL

*Definition, rationality, and structure are ways of seeing, but
they become prisons when they blank out other ways of seeing.*

—A. R. AMMONS (AMERICAN POET, 1926–2001)

*T*here is no question that science is extremely important in the advancement of human knowledge and progress. One of the greatest intellectual achievements of the human mind is how modern science enables the understanding of the laws and principles by which the universe is constructed and functions. Historically, science has been helpful in freeing people from the excesses of religious zeal, the arbitrary dictates of superstition, and wrongly held views that otherwise would have perpetuated much hardship. Scientific developments are occurring at an exponential rate in many areas, propelling the world's economies to higher levels of material living.

However, while humanity is to be congratulated for its collective genius, we should not become mesmerized by the apparent power of our invented tools but keep their value in proper perspective. William A. Tiller, Ph.D., author and professor emeritus of materials science and engineering at Stanford University, has pointed out how in the larger scheme of things:

> Our physical science does not necessarily deal with reality, whatever that is. Rather it has merely generated a set of consistency relationships to explain our common ground of experience . . . We have developed the mathematical laws based ultimately on a set of definitions of mass, charge, space, and time. We don't really know what these qualities are, but we have defined them to have certain unchanging properties and have thus constructed our edifice of knowledge on these pillars.[1]

WHEN SCIENCE BECOMES RELIGION

*Whoever undertakes to set himself up as a Judge of Truth and Knowledge is
shipwrecked by the laughter of the gods.*

—ALBERT EINSTEIN

Some scientists have the narrow view that science is the only justifiable
path to the truth, as if it were a new religion—a view known as scientism.
However, while science is an extremely useful tool, it is not the only path
to truth and should not displace or invalidate other areas of human in-
quiry and experience. For example, mystical traditions, which draw from
millennia of human intuitive experience, offer metaphysical insights that
scientism would dismiss as unprovable but which, nevertheless, enlighten
us about various dimensions of human existence. Underscoring this point,
professor of physics and humanities and scholar of Hindu religion, V. V.
Raman, suggests that an unfortunate consequence of the success of science
is its addiction to rationality,[2] while sages of the past realized the world is
far too complex to put everything in the straitjacket of reason. Further, the
limitations of the rational scientific view have been articulated by scholar
Jung Young Lee:

> We live in a broken world . . . [sensing] alienation of ourselves from
> reality . . . [while seeking] our identity. Gigantic machines overshadow
> human existence . . . [making us] insecure and afraid of growing dehu-
> manization . . . [while] Scientific technology has brought us comfort it
> has robbed our souls. Western civilization is one-sided not taking mysti-
> cal experiences seriously as essential aspects of human growth. Since man
> himself is mysterious, he cannot live without mystery.[3]

We have created a civilization in which many people feel that reason and
scientific data overshadow our intuition and spiritual qualities—trapping
us in a world based primarily on analysis, quantification, and mechanization.
This has resulted in cultural, religious, and spiritual practices being deni-
grated because they may not be scientifically provable, posing a pressing

dilemma since the greatest sense of fulfillment we feel as social and spiritual animals comes from such practices.

STRIKING A BALANCE

Treat the earth well,
It was not given to you by your parents,
It was loaned to you by your children.

—NATIVE AMERICAN PROVERB

To move forward for a better existence, we must strike a balance between acknowledging science and respecting the intuitive and spiritual nature of people. Having emerged from the cosmic soup as essentially intelligent monkeys who can type, we should recognize that we require a more holistic approach to life to meet our emotional, psychological, and spiritual needs. Science is an extremely useful tool for humankind, but it cannot provide a sense of fulfillment for creatures with social and spiritual dimensions. Albert Einstein warned, "It has become appallingly obvious that our technology has exceeded our humanity."[4] He went on to advise that "technological progress is like an axe in the hands of a pathological criminal."[5] When we have such power, we must be very careful how we wield it. It is just such technological delusions of grandeur that I believe might have prompted former American President John F. Kennedy to comment, "I am sorry to say that there is too much point to the wisecrack that life is extinct on other planets because their scientists were more advanced than ours."[6]

In addition to realizing the limitations of the scientific approach to provide for our needs, we must also be mindful not to let science and technology cause potentially irreversible damage to nature. Though science can provide many valuable solutions to environmental problems, when we believe that technology can solve all problems, we express hubris and behave as if we can do anything to the environment, contributing to the view that the environment is a consumable product. As biological organisms, we need air to breathe, water to drink, food to eat, and a place to live. While we need cash to buy these things in a market economy, cash is simply a proxy for those irreplaceable things. The two must not be confused.

The 2010 British Petroleum oil spill in the Gulf of Mexico demonstrated unequivocally how the damage we do to the "web of life" using technology can harm us and underscores the dangers of betting too much on supposedly fail-safe technology. Global warming provides another reminder of how fragile our environment really is and how imprudent it is to be reckless in the hope that technology might bail us out. Instead, humility and a more holistic view of nature should guide our actions as they did our ancestors.

While it is important to continue employing science for human advancement, we should do so with the greatest respect for the social, psychological, and spiritual needs of people. We need poetry, music, and art. We need to laugh, to cry, to occasionally fight, and to live and work together. We should be able to freely reach out to one another and other creatures in a healthy way that allows us to express our humanity. We must do this with a more holistic view of our existence that respects differing perspectives and balances the impact of the scientific view with the requirements of human nature. This approach should allow us to move forward while cherishing and protecting the spiritual and social side of human nature that makes life worthwhile.

Chapter 10

THE TECHNOLOGY TRAP

The system of nature, of which man is a part, tends to be self-balancing, self-adjusting, self-cleansing. Not so with technology.

—E. F. SCHUMACHER, *SMALL IS BEAUTIFUL*

*A*lthough technological advances have, in many ways, made our modern life easier and more comfortable, they have also created artificial environments that do not always support our social and spiritual needs. When computers were invented, they were employed primarily by universities and businesses for data processing. Today, they are widely used for communication. People now spend less time in the face-to-face social world and more time absorbed in artificial environments such as digital media. Despite the benefits of such technology, we must be aware of the often unintended negative impacts of it on a society over time.

In *Understanding Media: The Extensions of Man*, Canadian media guru Marshall McLuhan warned in the 1960s that we should be wary of new technological developments since they can alter human perception in subtle ways, perhaps causing harm, saying, "In a culture like ours, long accustomed to splitting and dividing all things as a means of control, it is sometimes a bit of a shock to be reminded that, in operational and practical fact, *the medium is the message.*"[1] [Emphasis added] To minimize the impacts of new technologies on society, we need to anticipate and take action to curtail them. Following McLuhan's advice, this chapter examines some of the impacts of recent technological developments on people so we might be more aware of them and consider how to counter any negative effects in the future.

FAKING EXPERIENCE

*Technology is the knack of arranging the world
so you don't have to experience it.*

—MAX FRISCH

To better understand the effects of new technologies today, we can focus on the "message" given us by observing the behavior of individuals who use computers and personal devices extensively. For parents, the scenario of several children sitting together and texting each other rather than interacting directly—teaching them to interact with technology and not with one another—is cause for concern.

In a worldwide academic study, students use words like *addicted, depressed, irritable,* and *crazy* to describe their reaction to being completely disconnected from their cell phones, computers, and portable music players for 24 hours.[2] The study showed that disconnection from such technology created a withdrawal reaction akin to that experienced when breaking an addiction to drugs or alcohol, indicating such people had a technology dependency and lost their sense of self when unplugged. In particular, smartphones have created dependency in people who use them, with a recent survey revealing that 65 percent of Canadians say they feel "naked" without the device and 82 percent admitting they use them while in the bathroom.[3] Technology experts predict further that the future will be fraught with "nomophobia," the fear of being out of mobile contact.

An even more specific example of how new technology is impacting us is how smartphones and texting are transforming our social mores, making it more difficult to tell lies or be flaky. Professor Richard Ling from the IT University of Copenhagen suggests people are in the grip of a new sociological phenomenon of "microcoordination"—where forms of verbal communication have given way to texting and other forms of media such as social media postings, which result in it being much easier to discover "white lies."[4] Similarly, according to Jodi R. R. Smith, president of the etiquette firm Mannersmith, such technology magnifies behavior, making it much easier to be aware of silliness and observe how . . . "those with bad manners now have glaringly bad manners."[5]

In examining these responses to technological devices, it is evident that while they have provided more freedom in some respects, in other ways, they have made people feel less free.

DIGITAL REALITIES

Virtual reality is like mainlining television.

—WILLIAM GIBSON

Virtual reality—created in computer cyberspace where a real or imaginary environment is simulated and users interact with and manipulate that world—is utilized beneficially in such areas as medicine, education, architecture, and entertainment. However, one clear harmful impact of virtual reality is that it is used by a growing number of people to escape from the actual into a fictional world—in effect, becoming a new kind of "opium for the masses."[6] For example, virtual worlds like Second Life and the World of Warcraft each have more than 10 million users who spend about 20 hours a week in an alternate reality.[7] People focused on such virtual reality can isolate themselves socially in the real world and become addicted to the medium, neglecting their basic self-interests and, in some cases, experiencing a kind of physical, emotional, and social retardation.

Recently, European scientists conducted research with adolescent video gamers that suggested gaming may be correlated to changes in the brain, much as addictions.[8] Concern is growing that such games may lead to abandoning real relationship responsibilities, instead, seeking the risk-free social hookups of the virtual world.[9] English author and philosopher Roger Scruton suggests that we might be witnessing a new kind of addiction, where something beneficial but hard to obtain in the real world is ". . . provided with a cost-free substitute, obtainable with the flick of a switch."[10] In the real world, such benefits come with important learning experiences that teach trust, accountability, and risk-taking, all of which are bypassed in virtual reality. There is also concern that excessive focus on virtual reality can result in a lack of authentic experiences, diminished opportunities to practice virtues such as courage, leading to and thus supporting a selfishly hedonistic lifestyle that does not require facing life's problems so people just drop out of the real world in favor of a less-challenging reality.[11]

MEDIA IMMERSION

All media exist to invest our lives with artificial
perceptions and arbitrary values.

—MARSHALL MCLUHAN

The sheer amount of time many people spend immersed in virtual reality and related digital media, and thus, absent from real social and natural environments, actually means losing years of their lives. According to the A.C. Nielsen Co., the average American watches more than 4 hours of TV each day (or 28 hours per week, or 2 months of nonstop TV-watching per year). The average home in the United States has the TV on for 6 hours, 47 minutes in a day, and collectively, Americans annually watch TV for a total of 250 billion hours.[12] Further, a recent consumer survey released by IBM suggested that people now spend as much or more time online as they do watching TV.[13] In the lifespan of 65 years, such people will have spent 9 years glued to the tube, more than enough time to earn a couple of university degrees.[14]

When you consider the time most people spend isolated from social and natural environments while sitting in front of computer monitors, texting, playing computer games, listening to audio devices, or in vehicles or controlled building environments, it is not surprising that we are losing touch with the real, tangible world and with one another.

NATURE DEFICIT AND SOCIAL ISOLATION

Social isolation is one of the most devastating
things you can do to a human being . . .

—ROSALIND WISEMAN (EXPERT ON HOST OF FAMILY RELATIONSHIP MATTERS)

The fact that the impact of modern media harmfully isolates humans from their natural environment and from direct contact with each other is causing alarm bells to ring for what author Richard Louv refers to as "nature-deficit disorder." While this term does not represent an existing medical diagnosis, he explains: "Nature-deficit disorder describes the human costs of alienation from nature which includes diminished use of the senses, attention difficulties, and higher rates of physical and emotional illness."[15]

As our separation from nature grows, we also physically separate more from one another. Nancy Dess, senior scientist with the American Psychological Association, suggests that since new communication technologies do not involve human touch, they place us one step removed from direct experience[16] and can lead to problems in the workplace and schools, where people are often forbidden, or at least discouraged, from any kind of physical contact. One potential implication Dess points out is that without touch, infant primates die and adult primates become more aggressive. Studies show that touch is essential to the peace-making process. Finally, Dess also believes that lack of touch contributes to violence in an ever-more tightly wired society.[17]

Given these harmful impacts on society by technological advances, we must look for how to strike a balance between the benefits of technology and modern media and the negative social and environmental impacts they may have. In particular, even though the new media provides people an easy way to "stay in touch," where people require actual physical and social touch, such media have the potential for exacerbating problems of spiritual disconnectedness and loneliness. T. S. Eliot's description of television as ". . . a medium of entertainment which permits millions of people to listen to the same joke and at the same time remain lonesome"[18] is instructive as to how a technology can simultaneously deliver a shared experience, great convenience, and possibly harmful isolation. In a world where we are increasingly conditioned to stay tuned into such media, we also need to find time to tune into each other directly and into the ultimate primordial media—nature.

Chapter 11

COMMON DOG FXXK

*Common sense is an uncommon degree
of what the world calls wisdom.*

—**Samuel Taylor Coleridge**

*T*oday, while the stock of technology has gone up, it has gone down for common sense, for which, I learned, while a commercial fisherman, there are many expressions, as the title for this chapter suggests. This chapter will examine the impacts of contemporary trends on the notion of common sense.

UNCOMMON SENSE

*It is common sense to take a method and try it. If it fails, admit
it frankly and try another. But above all, try something.*

—FRANKLIN D. ROOSEVELT

While technological breakthroughs have altered perceptions and the manner in which we communicate with one another,[1] people's diminishing contact with the real world and social isolation created by the use of new technology and media appear to be contributing to a growing lack of common sense.

The *Concise Oxford Dictionary* defines common sense as: "Normal understanding, good practical sense in everyday affairs, general feeling (of mankind or community)."[2] In this regard, philosopher and entrepreneur Greg Millbank, has said:

> The term "common sense" arises out of the Latin "sensus communis" which means roughly "the feelings we have in common." Seen from the perspective of human activity, such feelings are shared habits, that is,

77

they are habitual responses to certain situations which are familiar to the group. Common sense statements are therefore statements or thoughts about the best ways of doing things discovered by the group in their daily activities. Common sense is therefore nothing more or less than a collection of best and most universal habits of effective collaboration. It is a set of prescriptions for behavior generated out of collective experience . . .[3]

So common sense is, in effect, the patterns of shared experience of a group that evolve over time and become recognized as fundamental ideas that contribute to continued well-being and self-preservation.

For example, a recent poll found that "almost half of all Canadians are not able to complete basic skills, including installing a faucet or replacing a zipper," and 28 percent don't know how to change a tire[4]—abilities considered by our parents' generation as necessary to exceed the "idiot threshold."

One problem with losing common sense is that few people today are learning practical skills, while people routinely mastered them in the past as a part of commonsense knowledge and for self-preservation.

Another problem with losing common sense is that, as when we lose cultures, we then lose our most valuable practical database—the very encyclopedia of commonly held knowledge that ensures we do not continue to do stupid things that might ultimately impact our survival as a species.

If, due to excessive use of the new media, people no longer have a community with which to share habitual responses to certain situations, over time, the database of known experiences that represented past understandings of what common sense was will disappear. Lack of common sense to guide actions in the real world can then lead to confusion about what is actually possible and obscure hidden risks. This is reflected in the following blog one blogger recently posted:

> My husband caught our 12 year old walking on the [thin ice of a] frozen pond. When he yelled at her [to warn her of the danger], she said, "my boots are water proof [sic]." It never occurred to her that she could have fallen through and died. Now at almost 13 she isn't allowed outside in the winter unattended.[5]

Similarly, as a karate instructor for many years, I have seen the disconnect between youth brought up on martial arts action movies and video games and the brutal reality of fighting. Many think that fighting is like a video game, where heroes through glorified violence and hip-fighting techniques vanquish enemy characters without any apparent harmful consequences and are surprised when they experience the ramifications of fighting in the real world. One day a teenager came into my dojo (gym) to practice, dressed like Rambo in a muscle shirt, army fatigue pants, and a stylish bandana. The first time he was hit he had a look of utter horror and confusion on his face. To his surprise, getting hit in the real world wasn't anything like the movies, video games, or the highly choreographed techniques of pro-wrestling, but hurt for real.

Another scenario where confusion about reality led to a lack of common sense was when my former business partner in the commercial fishing industry hired an inexperienced deckhand who had trouble coping. In the middle of a raging storm at night when each gigantic wave threatened to smash the boat to pieces, this deckhand revealed his lack of common sense. While lying in a bunk in the fo'c'sle, seemingly oblivious to the fact that the vessel was being threatened by a storm miles from landfall, he asked my partner to stop and let him off the boat because he was terribly seasick—as if, like in a computer game, the fury of nature could be put on pause so that he could have a little break from it.

An interesting example of the interplay of common sense and people's reactions to new media in the past is the response of the 1903 Texas audience to the movie *The Great Train Robbery*.[6] There was a scene in which a cowboy aimed, then fired, his pistol directly into the camera so it appeared to those in the audience that they were being shot at. The audience responded in horror, running out of the theatre, having confused the new film medium with reality where getting shot could result in injury or death.

Interestingly, being from a different era, my grandmother would have a similar type of reaction when watching action drama on television. For example, she would be so engrossed when watching a murder mystery where a bad character would be sneaking up on an unsuspecting person that she would yell such things at the television as, "Turn around, stupid, he is right behind you. Look out, for God's sake, look out"—reactions that caused expressions of mirth among my siblings and I. Though such responses might be laughable to modern people accustomed to immersion in more advanced forms of media and technology, this reflects the confusion experienced by people coming from the real world, where common sense dictated that the result of having a gun pointed at you and fired was that you might be seriously injured or shot dead.

However, today, with so much gun violence and mayhem in mass and virtual media, the opposite problem exists—people have the tendency to become desensitized to violence through experiencing virtual violence and its lack of consequences and confuse their reactions with those when experiencing violence in the real world. When people become desensitized in this manner, it can lead to real violence and potential shock that the reality of pointing a gun and blasting a hole in a person's body is nothing like dispatching a virtual character—it is messy and bloody and comes with bothersome moral and legal consequences. Research on television violence, where there are three to five violent acts per hour during prime time viewing, and 20 to 25 violent acts per hour during children's Saturday morning programming, suggests such conditioning can lead directly to increased expressions of aggression in viewers.[7] Similar research suggests that exposure to violent video games also increases interpersonal aggression.[8]

The social isolation created by new technology and media that contributes to a growing lack of common sense can also result in irreparable damage to the real environment, our social relations, and possibly our physical well-being. Metaphorically, people in Western society are closer to becoming more like the 12-year-old girl on thin ice who, in the face of great peril, responded when warned of the danger by saying, "Don't worry, my boots are water proof." They often lack common sense and are unable to correctly assess the potential causes and effects of conditions. We need to gain awareness of such disconnects and interact more directly with nature and community to retain common sense.

Chapter 12

FUNNEL VISION

I am a red man. If the Great Spirit had desired me to be a
white man he would have made me so in the first place.
He put in your heart certain wishes and plans, in my heart
he put other and different desires. Each man is good in
his sight. It is not necessary for Eagles to be Crows.

—**SITTING BULL, HUNKPAPA SIOUX**

*W*hen people make judgments that the culture and practices of one's own society are "normal" and "natural," while those of other societies—because they are different—are abnormal and inferior, they exhibit an ethnocentrism that reflects narrow-mindedness.[1] Such ethnocentric tendencies exist in all cultures; however, because America has had such a dominant role in shaping the impact of global affairs, American ethnocentrism has been disproportionate.

In joking about American ethnocentrism, humorist Dave Barry said, "Americans who travel abroad for the first time are often shocked to discover that, despite all the progress that has been made in the last thirty years, many people continue to speak foreign languages."[2] This joke provides an example of the narrow view, or "tunnel vision," Americans often have when assessing other cultures—which I call "funnel vision" because the term more accurately describes the combination of such narrow vision with the disproportionate impact American culture has on the rest of the world—spreading its effect from the narrow tunnel to the widening mouth much like a funnel.

Western culture tends to judge technologically poor societies as inferior. It is reasoned that since their technology is deficient, their social, cultural, and spiritual practices are also inferior. But it does not necessarily follow that a society that is materially deficient or technologically unsophisticated is culturally or spiritually lacking.

81

For this reason, they should be respected and considered repositories of knowledge from which people can learn more about the human condition, rather than dismissed. Take, for example, the early Western view of the Chinese culture as reflected in the *I Ching*, the oldest and most important of the Chinese Confucian classic texts considered to have at its roots the very foundation of Chinese civilization. It is not a religious book but rather a wisdom book, not simply a book of philosophy but a book of art as well, which grew out of ancient oracles. For the Chinese, divination has nothing to do with the divine or the supernatural but is a search for decisions in relation to action—the very purpose of wisdom in a highly practical culture.[3] The great sophistication and value of the *I Ching* was initially misunderstood by those in the West and pronounced insane and heretical by Jesuit missionaries in the seventeenth century.[4]

As Western nations expanded throughout the world, they applied a similar narrow ethnocentric focus to other cultures and civilizations. If foreign societies didn't reflect European customs or technology, they were simply considered inferior and fair targets for assimilation. The problem with this kind of narrow-minded thinking is that it devalues the vast human cultural pool that is potentially the greatest source of knowledge available to humankind. Every culture holds some valuable insights for others. Cultures are not just important but critical to the well-being of people because they represent millennia of knowledge acquired from unique geographic and environmental conditions—providing alternative and distinctive adaptation strategies for survival.

INVESTING IN CULTURE

The only thing worse than being blind is having sight but no vision.

—HELEN KELLER

A narrow ethnocentric focus was also possessed by early colonizers of what is now the United States. By 1890, European nations bent on expanding their power across America impacted the Native American tribes, annihilating ". . . a majority of several hundred distinct cultures that flourished in North America before the arrival of Columbus and had pushed to the edge of extinction most of the remaining tribal groups."[5] Just as with the early Western view of the *I Ching*, people bent on colonizing new territories did not look beyond their ethnocentric blinders to see the value and wisdom in the views of the various indigenous populations.

Unfortunately, there still remains a tendency in American society to belittle or discount the value of any culture that is different or has less-developed technology. They are considered interesting subjects for academics to study but which have little to offer the modern world.

Horace Miner, a professor emeritus of sociology and anthropology at the University of Michigan, brilliantly satirized this tendency in a 1956 paper titled "Body Ritual among the Nacirema." In this paper, published in the *American Anthropologist*, he mocked the cultural conceit of American society writing about the strange and intriguing North American tribe known as the "Nacirema."[6] The Nacirema were consumed by ritual activity relating to the body and its appearance and health.[7] Miner wrote, "The fundamental belief underlying the whole system appears to be that the human body is ugly and that its natural tendency is to debility and disease."[8] This fascinating undiscovered tribe apparently lived in the territory between the Canadian Cree, the Yaqui, and Tarahumare of Mexico, and the Carib and Arawak of the Antilles (essentially within the continental United States).[9]

What transpired as a result of the article was akin to Orson Welles's 1938 radio drama *The War of the Worlds,* which created widespread panic when people thought a program about aliens invading the earth was real. Many readers of Miner's article, including numerous anthropologists, thought it really described a new indigenous tribe, not understanding that Nacirema is actually "American" spelled backward. What Miner was actually describing in anthropological jargon was American culture of the 1950s. Miner's point was that applying such stilted language of anthropology to American culture made it appear just as foreign and backward as the "primitive" cultures that Americans looked down on.

Once one understands the article is a spoof, it is amusing to read as is evident from the following excerpt:

> There are ritual fasts to make fat people thin and ceremonial feasts to make thin people fat. Still other rites are used to make women's breasts larger if they are small and smaller if they are large. General dissatisfaction with breast shape is symbolized in the fact that the ideal form is virtually outside the range of human variation. A few women afflicted with almost superhuman hyper mammary development are so idolized that they make a handsome living by simply going from village to village and permitting the natives to stare at them for a fee.[10]

It is not surprising that many Americans were confused and felt indignation when their culture was portrayed in the way that academics typically describe other so-called primitive cultures,[11] experiencing the type of resentment familiar to non-Western civilizations and indigenous groups who have long been the subjects of such studies.

It is important that this kind of ethnocentric hubris does not blind us to the inherent values, knowledge, and wisdom contained within other cultures. It serves no purpose to be willfully blind to the social, spiritual, and intellectual sophistication of less materially or technologically advanced cultures when their practices might hold valuable lessons. For our future well-being, we should be mindful of Charles Darwin's observation that it is not the fittest who survive but those *most adaptable to change.*[12] Certainly with the collective wisdom of all cultures, we might ensure that we have the best knowledge available to adapt to a rapidly changing world.

SAVING OUR CULTURAL LEGACY

When the well is dry, we know the worth of water.

—BENJAMIN FRANKLIN

Mahatma Gandhi commented that "No culture can live if it attempts to be exclusive."[13] I believe it was anthropologist Margaret Mead who said something to the effect that if we are not careful, we may wake up one morning and forget that there is another way to live besides our own way of life. The vast pool of knowledge existing in the world's cultures is perhaps more important to the survival of Homo sapiens than having a broad gene pool.

What is lost with the death of a culture is an invaluable legacy of knowledge and wisdom relating to harmonious human relations, the environment, and how millennia of accumulated human insight can provide direction for a society. A good example of the valuable use of such knowledge is the recent recognition of Australian Aborigine plant knowledge in predicting future weather patterns. In an effort to understand and forecast droughts in Australia, weather forecasters have belatedly recognized ancient Aboriginal knowledge accumulated from over 40,000 years of experience.[14]

Unfortunately, we have done and continue to do an unsettlingly efficient job of wiping out cultures. In my own tribal village of Lax Kw'alaams, we are rapidly losing our elders, a situation that, combined with the dominant force of popular media, bodes poorly for the Tsimshian culture. When we lose them, we don't just lose speakers of the language but guides to the cosmogony of our culture, tellers of our stories and myths, individuals who can connect us with the collected ancient wisdom of our people and with our identity as Tsimshians. When elders pass away, the pulse of our culture gets weaker, and we lose the 13,000-year connection to rich, complex, Canadian northwest coast arts and traditions. We lose a unique worldview and language with subtle and evocative ways of expressing ideas that do not exist in the English language.

Author Wade Davis warns that we are living through a period in which incredibly half of humanity's cultural legacy is being lost in a single generation.[15] According to another source, of the nearly six thousand languages in the world, half are in decline and only 10 percent are expected to survive the century.[16] In Canada, for example, 70 percent of the indigenous languages are in decline, causing one elder to comment, "It's like watching animals go extinct."[17] If language is the soul of the culture, it will be impossible for a culture to survive without the language that articulates its thoughts and ideas.

In losing language, we also lose the oral traditions of tribal cultures throughout the world renowned for their beautiful expressions of mythic stories and mystic imagery. Will we ever again hear the dazzling oratory of the likes of Red Jacket, Chief Seattle, Red Cloud, Sitting Bull, Big Elk, or Cochise? Will we also lose the beautiful spiritual legacy of tribes of the Canadian northwest coast?

Most people realize that the ancient Greek civilization spanned nearly two thousand years until it was overtaken by the Roman Empire in the second century BCE. However, what many individuals do not know is that, like many indigenous cultures, the Greeks had no form of writing and, therefore, had an oral culture until about the eighth century BC. Up until then, Greek stories and history were handed down through each generation by word of mouth—in precisely the same manner as most indigenous cultures. It is interesting to speculate about how much cultural knowledge and traditions would have been lost—no doubt the very foundation of Western society—if the Roman Empire had overtaken Greek civilization 600 years earlier, when Greek culture had been based on oral tradition, and applied the same cultural hubris that Westerners apply to indigenous and other cultures, devaluing or destroying Greek culture.

In this regard, it is fortunate that the Maori culture and language of New Zealand are still very much alive. One of my Maori friends, Te Taru White, can still orally recite his genealogy from ancestor to ancestor for the 700-year period from the first arrival of their beautiful *wakas* (oceangoing canoes) in Aotearoa, the Maori name for New Zealand, which means "land of the long white cloud."

If, as Oscar Wilde suggested, "Experience is simply the name we give our mistakes,"[18] what we lose when cultures disappear is our most valuable practical database, the experiences and unique perspectives that have evolved over time—the very encyclopedia of cultural knowledge that could ensure we make the most informed choices as a species.

Memory of the Ancestors
(Maori Leader Te Taru White)

Sadly, with the loss of indigenous or any cultural knowledge, the complex web of ancient wisdom relating to our adaptability simply vanishes into the ether of the cosmos, akin to stripping human beings of the most valuable intellectual and experiential weapons needed for their survival.

In this way, we lose the unique understanding of nature, human relation-ships, social organization, cooperation, and critical social skills necessary for social harmony and happiness. We also forfeit the understanding of seasonal change and relationships among species and environments that enable people to manage their resources. While we are exponentially gaining technological knowledge, we are, at an equally astonishing pace, losing our most important cultural legacy as a species—the diverse knowledge critical to developing social skills across generations, families, communities, societies, and philosophies. With the loss of indigenous cultures, are we also losing the cultural mind-set for having a profound respect and caring for all things as mere strands in "the web of life"? Have we already lost views that could be informing a much more careful approach to the environment and the biosphere? Surely, such traditional ecological knowledge, and the values it engenders, are highly relevant today. By chance, the cosmos delivered Ishi to modern history, providing a valuable glimpse of what such a terrible loss to mankind the eradication of Yahi culture has been. Hopefully, we are not doomed to repeat our mistakes on a much-grander scale.

PART III

Creating Harmony

COSMIC BALANCE

Children laugh
Birds sing
Family together.

People see
Sad earth
Great care.

Village works
Dogs bark
Good dependency.

Understanding
Twinkling star
Humble heart.

Grandma cries
Orca leaps
Proper place.

Modest wants
Eagle soars
Self-reliance.

Baby sings
Wolves howl
Seeing true.

Sharing all
Kitten meows
Joining hands.

Father helps
Raven croaks
All belong.

Rituals rise
Growling bear
Growing peace.

Chapter 13

BALANCING ACT

*Wakan Tanka, Great Mystery, teach me how to trust my heart,
my mind, my intuition, my inner knowing, the senses of my body,
the blessings of my spirit. Teach me to trust these things so
that I may enter my Sacred Space and love beyond my fear, and
thus Walk in Balance with the passing of each glorious Sun.*

—**LAKOTA PRAYER**

*W*e have created a society that is not only wreaking havoc on our culture and environment but is also seriously harming our social and spiritual well-being. When changes seep into the psyche over a long period of time, it is understandable that we lose our ability to recognize the harm they may cause. However, once we are aware of such damage and understand how our perspectives have been altered by circumstances over time and how they impact our long-term well-being, we have no excuse for continuing on the same path and every reason for seeking a better way forward. Upon becoming president, Lyndon B. Johnson once famously said, when briefly considering firing FBI Director J. Edgar Hoover, "I would rather have him inside the tent pissing out than outside the tent pissing in."[1] When we choose to remain willfully blind to self-inflicted injury, we are essentially pissing inside our own tent.

Our economic model has become a self-imposed trap where the bait is mindless consumption and, for governments, the near-term illusion of prosperity. In developing a society focused primarily on materialism, we have been imbued with the conceit that we are above other forms of life, unwittingly separating ourselves from nature and its social and spiritual healing powers. Our precious time and efforts are devoted to constantly working so we can consume things that are supposed to make us happy—yet we remain unfulfilled. The work-spend-debt cycle is contributing significantly to making people emotionally ill, while the debt-financed economic growth myth is unsustainable. If we truly want to dance with spirits, we must recognize the fundamental shortcomings of the society we have created.

Unfortunately, many people only discover in old age that a life spent simply amassing material possessions without greater purpose is an empty one. Existence should be much more than an exercise in accounting. It should be an experience where each of us, for the short time we are here, can find purpose in life and can enjoy the beauty, the love, and the wonder of human sharing and nature—experiences that should not be the exclusive province of innocent children or secluded monks.

I believe that in spite of the spiritual and social crisis sweeping Western societies, now there is reason for hope. We must, however, awaken from the slumber of materialism to find a way forward to happier, richer, and more fulfilling lives based also on supporting social and spiritual needs.

From time immemorial, experience has taught that we have deep social and spiritual longings that are simply part of our human nature. How often we feed this need determines the level of happiness we feel in life. In the end, it is of no consequence whether we can provide a scientific explanation for this necessity—we must simply accept that this is hardwired into our social and psychic DNA. Fundamental self-interest dictates we must throttle back on *Spaceship Earth* and see clearly the unsustainability of the current consumption and economic course, realizing that such a route is not only likely to exacerbate the spiritual and social drought that society is now experiencing but will unquestionably lead to considerably more hardship, especially for the poor and vulnerable in society.

In seeking constructive change, we must believe in the essential goodness of humanity and draw upon the ancient experience and wisdom of our ancestors. With such knowledge, we have to willfully alter our course to reflect our true place in the cosmos and our human requirements. With awareness of the kind of society we have created, we can move forward with a social and spiritual consciousness more attuned to our needs.

We can nurture the human desire to feel we truly belong somewhere and are loved. We can nourish our spirits in a way that sustains hope and continues to provide insight for our long-term survival as a species.

Part I and Part II of this book have examined the kind of society we have created and its impacts. Part III looks at constructive ways we might adjust our priorities and change our mind-set with a view to creating more balance, fulfilling more fundamental needs, and more readily seeing ourselves in a universal context. In reconnecting to the universe, we may once again experience nature's most gratifying gifts—blessings that flow to those attuned to its magnificent harmony.

Chapter 14

ECONOMIC REFORM FOR SOCIAL AND SPIRITUAL DIVIDENDS

Where is the Life we have lost in living?
Where is the wisdom we have lost in knowledge?
Where is the knowledge we have lost in information?

—T. S. ELIOT, *CHORUSES FROM "THE ROCK"*

*A*comical image from the war in Iraq was Foreign Minister Tariq Aziz giving an ill-timed interview to CNN on the streets of Baghdad during which he assured the world that there was no war afoot as large plumes of smoke rose behind him from bombs dropped by American warplanes. False assertions as to the soundness of our economic model from economists, bankers, and government representatives which seem to belie reality resemble that of the hapless Tariq Aziz. However, such assurances are not comical against the backdrop of the Great Recession of 2008, the ongoing European debt crisis, and the unrest of the Arab Spring and the Occupy Movement.

While the current economic model focusing on consumption, materialism, and wealth has raised living standards in the short term, the fact that it has had harmful social and spiritual impacts on the population needs to be recognized and addressed.

AN ECONOMIC MODEL BASED ON MONEY MANIA

Money is like an iron ring we put through our nose. It
is now leading us around wherever it wants. We just
forgot that we are the ones who designed it.

—MARK KINNEY

Over time, people have been conditioned to believe that money—the currency of consumption—doesn't just count but is the only thing worth striving for and that the value of everything should be measured by it. Lynne Twist, author of *The Soul of Money*,[1] argues that people have lost any sensible perspective on money and are in a literal craze about it. She contends that we have now made money more important than human life, the natural world, and our own spirituality, and should return to a life where money and the pursuit of material possessions are put in their proper place—behind spiritual and social objectives, such as meaningful relationships and genuine stewardship.[2]

The current economic model has elevated money above its true role as a proxy to provide for our needs as biological, social, and spiritual creatures. Instead of treating money as a simple medium of exchange, we confuse its value with the real items we actually need to exist. Money is a useful medium of exchange but otherwise intrinsically worthless since it can't be eaten, drunk, or used to provide shelter. Twist notes: ". . . [while we] relate to money as if it is fact of nature, a force to be reckoned with . . . [it has] no more inherent power than a notepad or a Kleenex, [and] has become the single most controlling force in our lives."[3]

We have lost sight of the fact that in itself, money is neither good nor bad and has no inherent authority. It is we who give money its power, and, since it is a human invention, we also have the authority to change this to suit our evolving needs so we do not unwittingly become slaves to our own creation.

In giving money such a high priority, we have forgotten that once basic needs are provided for, happiness primarily arises from relationships with family, friends, and community; feeling we are contributing to and valued by these groups; and having a true life's purpose. And yet, when faced with the social and spiritual fallout from a system that focuses our attention on consumption and material possession, we profess to be mystified as to why this is happening.

It is also worth noting again that the debt-based Western economic model driven by interest payments is a practice that is opposed to a sustainable economy, focusing our attention on immediate rather than long-term objectives. People need to understand that at least 50 percent of all labor goes to pay for interest charges on the collective outstanding debt throughout the economy,[4] a fact that places the yoke of economic dependency on everyone. We need to explore other practical alternatives to banking and currency systems, such as the credit union concept, for instance, the no-interest credit union concept exemplified by the JAK Members Bank of Sweden,[5] and Local Exchange Transaction Systems (LETS).[6]

Instead of considering ways to alter our perspective on and valuing of money and material possessions, people have been conditioned to accept the economic model as simply a fact of modern life—"just the way it is"— foolishly enslaving ourselves to it, rather than gaining control over it. This may be partly due to the fact that our current economic model has developed in society incrementally, making its impacts less perceptible to many people and making individuals unable to comprehend it. What most observers do not realize is that the economic model and the mind-set it promotes have arisen only recently. Historically, there were good reasons for having a very different view of the role of economics and for not assessing everything in monetary terms. Such views and reasons will be examined in the following chapter.

In addition, it is critical to understand how, over the last couple hundred years, marketplaces have given way to market economies,[7] which have come to govern every aspect of our lives. Political philosopher Michael J. Sandel points out how we are now living in a society where everything is for sale—social, civic, and government services and functions—items that were previously off-limits to the marketplace. In other words, with the shift (begun with Thatcher and Reagan) to the era of market triumphalism (arrogant confidence in the validity and success of markets), we drifted from having a market economy to being a market society with a corresponding change in values.

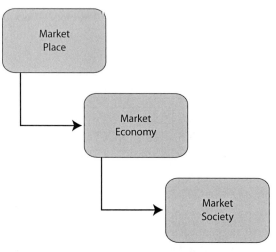

FIGURE 20 *Evolution of Market in Western Society*

Having a market economy has been a good thing because it is the most effective mechanism to date for organizing the production and distribution of goods and generating affluence and prosperity. However, having a market society in which markets determine everything does not take into account the social and spiritual needs of people, and can lead, among other impacts, to inequality and corruption. When we artificially make money the measure of everything, we ignore and denigrate those intangible but invaluable things important to people that cannot be measured by money.

In seeking to understand why modern people are experiencing such horrendous spiritual and social problems, it is worthwhile to examine the attitudes of past cultures and religions toward those focused on wealth and money. Previously, it was thought that economics alone should not shape societies, as it largely does today—that societies had more important objectives.

Chapter 15 focuses on the reasons why many past societies felt it was important to moderate the impact of money and economics by giving them a lower priority than social and spiritual needs.

Chapter 15

HISTORICAL WISDOM

The guidance we need . . . cannot be found in science or technology, the value of which utterly depends on the ends they serve; but it can still be found in the traditional wisdom of mankind.

—E. F. SCHUMACHER, *SMALL IS BEAUTIFUL*

*N*owadays, the notion of wealth is inevitably associated with money, material possessions, and power, but in many societies and traditions, accumulating excessive wealth and material goods was seen as either undesirable for spiritual growth or unnecessary for well-being and ethical living. In Old English, the word *wealth* was derived from combining *weal* (well-being) with *th* (condition)—meaning the "condition of well-being."[1] This usage of wealth could include money and material possessions but encompassed the intangible things that are important to people. Similarly, the Greek word for wealth is *euporeo, eu* meaning "well" and *poros* meaning "a passage"—that is, wealth was thought to be a way of being well.[2] Since Greek was the original language of the New Testament, this connotation of wealth has added importance for Christians.

The teachings of early Christianity warned explicitly of the spiritual pitfalls of focusing too much on acquiring material wealth. For example, in the Sermon on the Mount (Matthew 19:24), Jesus states, "And again I say unto you, it is easier for a camel to go through the eye of a needle, than for a rich man to enter into the kingdom of God." In other words, the more we pursue material gratification, the more difficult it is to find true spiritual salvation. Further, in Matthew 6:19–21, Jesus speaks directly against the universal human propensity to accumulate wealth and the impact this has on spiritual pursuits: "Do not store up for yourselves treasures on earth, where moths and vermin destroy, and where thieves break in and steal. But store up for yourselves treasures in heaven, where moths and vermin do not destroy, and where thieves do not break in and steal. For where your treasure is, there your heart will be also."

Finally, in Matthew 6:24, Jesus says, "No man can serve two masters: for either he will hate the one, and love the other; or else he will hold to the one, and despise the other. You cannot serve God and mammon," with the word *mammon* suggesting material wealth. Thus, Matthew 6:19 to 34 reminds us that to live a righteous life, we must deal wisely with wealth and material resources in ways which allow us to follow a spiritual path. Similarly, Catholic theologian St. Thomas Aquinas also had the view that genuine happiness required virtuous action and a sufficiency (not excess) of material goods.[3]

Ancient Chinese society reflected a similar perspective by placing merchants at the bottom of the social ladder—below scholars, bureaucrats, farmers, and artisans—because they did not produce anything that contributed to the good of the entire society. Working primarily for personal gain was seen as a characteristic of an inferior person (小人) and unethical. On the other hand, scholars were thought to provide knowledge for the common social good, farmers produced essential food and paid valuable land tax, and artisans made useful goods.

Further, historically, in China, the notion of *xiaokang* (小康) put forward by Confucius, which literally means "moderately well off," was used to describe a society consisting of a middle class of moderate affluence whose citizens were not in need.[4] China's former leaders Hu Jintao and Wen Jiabao committed China to the goal of building *xiaokang shehui*—a "moderately wealthy" society—by the year 2020.[5] Their view was that genuine well-being is best achieved when people have their material needs met, individuals are living lives of moderation, and material goods are equitably distributed to all.[6]

Moreover, economist Mark Anielski, author of *The Economics of Happiness*, points out how Europeans in the Middle Ages (from the fifth to the sixteenth century) sought a good life characterized by frugality and subsistence—similar to the modern concept of sustainability.[7] He also discusses how the ethics of ancient Israel was based on the view that people only had stewardship, not ownership, of wealth since, according to ancient Jewish philosophy, all wealth belonged to God.[8]

The historical literature on Native Americans is full of similar views. For example, Chief Red Cloud stressed that the focus of his people was not on acquiring material wealth but . . . "[training] our children right" and to living in "peace and love."[9] A Huichol holy man stated that "humankind must be a steward of the Earth."[10] An Oglala Sioux proverb cautions that we must treat the earth well (the source of all wealth for everyone) because it was not given to us by our ancestors but loaned to us by our children.[11]

As emphasized by these historical views and noted in my previous book *The Economic Dependency Trap*, once we have provided for our basic needs, money may increase our options for material comfort but does not necessarily lead to greater well-being. With this understanding and the view that the current consumption-based economic model is not sustainable, the following chapters explore possible constructive changes that might be made to achieve more balance, including:

- Creating a new definition of wealth and progress;
- Changing our perception of the economic model to recognize the unsustainable consumption occurring;
- Altering our economic model so it:
  - incorporates a sustainability measure
  - takes into account the social and spiritual nature of people
  - balances entrepreneurial free-for-all tendencies against social and corporate responsibility
  - emphasizes morality while keeping greed in check

Chapter 16

A NEW DEFINITION OF WEALTH AND PROGRESS

There is no wealth but life. Life including all of its powers of love, of joy, and of admiration. That country is richest which nourishes the greatest number of noble and happy human beings; that man is richest who, having perfected the functions of his own life to the utmost, has also the widest helpful influence, both personal, and by means of his possessions, over the lives of others.

—JOHN RUSKIN

*T*he current measurement of national well-being, the Gross Domestic Product (GDP),[1] the market value of all goods and services produced in a given period,[2] provides one way to compare the well-being of countries since it is measured frequently, widely, and consistently. However, as we have seen, GDP only gauges specific financial data and, thus, some aspects of well-being but not others. In 1968, Robert Kennedy lamented (just weeks before his untimely assassination) that while GDP was useful for reflecting the amount of money spent on goods and services, it was an imprecise measure of what mattered most to Americans: their quality of life.[3] The architects of the GDP, John Maynard Keynes (United Kingdom) and Simon Kuznets (United States), acknowledged its shortcomings in 1962 when Kuznets warned that "the welfare of a nation can scarcely be inferred from a measurement of national income as defined by GDP . . . goals for 'more' growth should specify of what and for what."[4]

Some important factors that GDP does not reflect are:

- the fact that it sums up all financial transactions without accounting for costs
- the inequities in wealth distribution

- nonmarket transactions such as household production and volunteer or unpaid services while treating crime, imprisonment, divorce, and other forms of family and social breakdown as economic gain
- how it increases with each environmental calamity, and again, with every reconstruction activity
- depletion and degradation of natural resources and the environment
- the fact that it treats war expenditures as economic gain both during the destruction and rebuilding phases
- debt levels of a population or its governments
- the underground economy
- the value of assets in an economy
- sustainability of growth

As a result, GDP can paint a limited and misleading picture of a country's well-being. For example, with regard specifically to the United States, it does not reflect the enormous stress experienced by the population and the attendant outcomes, such as drug addiction and incarceration rates; personal and government debt burdens; the fact that the economic model is based entirely on consumption and is not sustainable; nor the enormous inequities in wealth distribution.

A recently suggested alternative indicator more reflective of the actual well-being of countries is the Genuine Progress Indicator (GPI).[5] The GPI is a more holistic measure of economic and general progress that starts with GDP and adjusts for unpaid work (volunteerism and housework) and a variety of other factors.[6] Using this measurement, the period from 1950 to 1995 revealed a startling trend in America: while both GPI and GDP increased in tandem until 1973, the GPI has since declined steadily, whereas the GDP has continued to rise, as illustrated in figure 21.[7]

In other words, if, taking the GDP approach, we simply sum up transactions in an economy without accounting for the benefits and costs of real wealth—natural, human, and social—we are left with a highly misleading

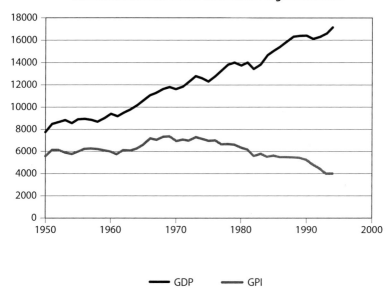

US Gross Domestic Product vs. Genuine Progress Indicator

—— GDP   —— GPI

FIGURE 21   *Growing Gulf Between Quality of Life and GDP*

index of well-being. The ultimate verdict on the legitimacy of the GDP as a measurement of well-being may well come in the form of civil disobedience that threatens to morph into widespread social explosions.

Further, there have been several other approaches to measuring economic progress that take into account other important factors to well-being, such as the Human Development Index, Gross National Happiness, Happy Planet Index, OECD Better Lives Dashboard, and Composite Wealth Indicators. One of the more interesting and comprehensive measures, advanced by Mark Anielski in his book *The Economics of Happiness*, is called Genuine Wealth (GW). GW means the conditions of well-being that are true to our core values of life and includes what people value most about life, such as love, meaningful relationships, happiness, joy, freedom, self-sufficiency, justice, and peace.[8] The GW model proposes a practical way to account for conditions of life that either contribute to or detract from our genuine well-being and GW, which can be assessed for individuals, communities, and national governments. It takes into consideration the following capital:

- human—individual minds, bodies, and spirits and their capabilities
- social—quality and strength of community relations, which encompass matters such as trust, honesty, common values, and tolerance
- natural—stocks and funds of things in nature that yield flows of natural resources and life-supporting ecosystems
- built—machines, tools, durable consumer goods
- financial—money and other liquid assets acceptable for payment of transactions and debts[9]

I believe there needs to be international dialog and agreement on a more holistic approach to determining the well-being and progress of countries. Such a new international standard might include measurement of such things as:

- GDP (with adjustments to include some financial items from the list of deficiencies on pages 105–106)
- Living standards
- Life expectancy
- Education levels
- Health levels and availability of healthcare
- Good governance
- Social and democratic freedoms
- Openness and transparency of government and institutions
- Quality of life issues
- Ecosystem diversity and resilience
- Environmental sustainability and compliance with international standards

- Treatment of nature's capital (forests, oil, gas, coal, water, and so forth) in the manner manufactured and produced capital (such as buildings, equipment, and so forth) are treated so that we may assess whether they have depreciated (been depleted or degraded) or appreciated (grown in value or quality)
- Cultural diversity and vitality
- Time use and balance
- Community vitality
- Psychological well-being
- Personal and government debt levels
- Wealth distribution

Perhaps such a new measurement of a nation's well-being might also be incorporated into an international standard of measurement, such as the International Organization for Standardization (ISO) system that exists to set international standards for business, government, and society. Of course, there would have to be agreement on what was to be measured and assurance that countries have the ability to measure those items correctly.

As well, to incentivize countries to seek a more holistic progress measurement there should be international annual awards established to recognize the achievers who are creating the prototype of sustainable society needed for humankind to survive in the long term—awards that define the "golden sustainability standard." Such awards might be called the Global Progress and Well-being Awards, and could be endorsed by such groups as the United Nations, the World Bank, and the International Monetary Fund, and hopefully capture the attention of global groups like the one which selects recipients of the Nobel Peace Prize. Such awards might recognize leaders who have made the most improvement in specific areas—like the greatest increase in wealth distribution, greatest improvement in environmental standards, and the greatest increase in population longevity.

Although such a proposal would require the agreement of many countries and institutions at a time when governments are scrambling to pay off enormous debts, at the very least, citizens and governments should begin to discuss such issues publicly with the goal of perhaps establishing an international forum for dialog about them that includes all nations and their key NGOs along the lines of the Davos World Economic Forum.

Dialog about and implementation of some or all of these possible changes and improvements could help us move forward to achieve greater well-being and more genuine wealth and progress based on a broader range of human needs and better wealth distribution.

Chapter 17

A NEW SOCIAL CONTRACT WITH A REBUILT ECONOMIC ENGINE

The day is not far off when the economic problem will take the back seat where it belongs, and the arena of the heart and head will be occupied or reoccupied, by our real problems—the problems of life and human relations, of creation and behavior and religion.

—JOHN MAYNARD KEYNES

$\mathcal{T}$he problem with the Western approach to economic development is that it is simply not sustainable. It is tied to natural resource use at a time when huge existing populations are adopting the same model, increasing the exploitation of limited resources and negatively impacting an already overtaxed environment. Future population growth will further diminish resources and create more environmental problems. We must acknowledge that the consumption-based economic model is unsustainable in the spirit of Charles Darwin's maxim that those survive who can best adapt to the realities of existence and seek a practical course of action forward.

This chapter looks at creating a sustainable economic model under a new social contract that delivers what people as social and spiritual animals need. This involves exposing the unrealistic expectations of perpetual economic growth, dealing with the debt trap created by the money supply system, and examining potential reforms more reflective of true well-being.

THE FAIRY TALE OF GROWTH FOREVER

Anyone who thinks that exponential growth can go on forever
in a finite world is either a madman or an economist.

—KENNETH BOULDING

As already pointed out, because people have to provide for basic needs to survive, some consumption is necessary, but with a potential world population of 15 billion by 2100 and the finite supply of natural resources, our current economic model, based on unbridled consumption and unending growth, is unsustainable.

As Professors Tim Jackson and Peter Victor from York University, Toronto, point out, "Every society clings to the myth by which it lives, and ours is the myth of economic growth."[1] They further note that for the last 5 decades, the pursuit of economic growth has been the single-most important policy objective around the world, with growth of the global economy over the last half century increasing fivefold, projecting that if it continues growing at the same rate, it will be 80 times larger by 2100, as illustrated in figure 22. They advise that this situation "is totally at odds with the scientific knowledge of the finite resource base and the fragile ecology on which we depend for survival, and has already led to degradation of an estimated 60 percent of the world's ecosystems."[2]

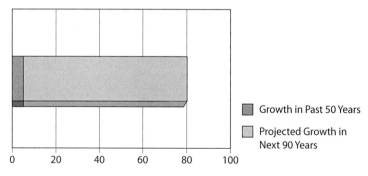

FIGURE 22 *Impossibility of Global Economic Growth Forever in a World of Finite Resources*

Once we have an understanding of how the economic model requires such high levels of growth to pay off escalating interest payments, however, it is possible to comprehend why this situation exists, although harder to grasp why we opt to continue down such a dead-end path when we can choose a wiser course.

The question of economic growth and the environment has largely put economists and ecologists into separate and opposing camps. Both are criticized for making extreme statements about the dangers posed and the positions of the other. On the one hand, there are compelling reasons for skepticism about allowing economic and population growth to continue unabated forever. On the other hand, there is similar skepticism toward ecologists and others in whose opinions "questioning growth is deemed to be the act of lunatics, idealists, and revolutionaries."[3] The climate, however, might now be changing, with France's former President Sarkozy, Nobel Prize–winning economist Joseph Stiglitz, and other respected international figures arguing that prosperity is now possible without GDP growth and may become impossible because of GDP growth. As well, in the aftermath of the recent global financial crisis, more people are questioning the mantra of "growth at all costs." Consequently, the time has come to consider the merits of a steady-state, subsistence economy that can achieve self-sufficiency and balance.

EFFECTING CHANGE IN TUMULTUOUS TIMES

The bamboo that bends is stronger than the oak that resists.

—JAPANESE PROVERB

How do we encourage people and governments to begin dialog about adopting a long-term sustainable economic model when the modern economy is structurally reliant on economic growth for its stability? Such a question is made more difficult to answer when politicians panic as growth falters, when businesses struggle to survive, when people lose jobs and homes, and recession looms.

We can begin by acknowledging that the current economic model is headed for a serious day of reckoning as a result of its unsustainability, with enormous potential repercussions for the well-being of everyone, examine what is not working with the current approach, and engage in dialog about what intelligent corrective measures we should take to mitigate the impact of the economic model.

We have already looked at the stress being placed on the population from debt obligations and growing economic, social, and spiritual deficits. The Occupy Movement and Arab Spring protestors have confirmed that it is not working for the 2 billion people who still live on less than $2 a day, for the masses of impoverished people in industrialized countries who are not receiving a fair share of wealth, and for a middle class feeling they are being squeezed out of existence having to support national GDP by buying on credit things they don't need.

In light of such developments, we need to question just how "civilized" a society is where prosperity is founded on ecological destruction and social injustice, especially in a world of finite resources and with the growing frustration of populations increasingly unable to tolerate such inequities.

Perceptions of such inequities are not being helped by insensitive behavior of the superrich. Take, for example, media reports highlighting the antics and obscene wealth of the world's richest woman, Australian Gina Rinehart, whose wealth is currently estimated at $32 billion (earning $51.5 million per day, or $645 per second) and is expected to rise to $104 billion in a country where the mistreated Aborigine population—on whose traditional lands her mining wealth is founded—eke out a meager existence and suffer some of the worst social pathologies on the planet. Now ordinary Australians are starting to criticize the superwealthy as: "A handful of vested interests that have pocketed a disproportionate share of the nation's economic success [who] now feel they have a right to shape Australia's future to satisfy their own self-interest . . . comparable to Russian oligarchs . . . who further feel they can behave however you like."[4] Such criticisms come close on the heels of the disgraceful conduct of the News Corp. empire, concerning a parliamentary report which concluded that megabillionaire Rupert Murdoch is "not a fit person" to run a huge media conglomerate in which widespread phone hacking was a common practice.[5] This scandal has touched the highest level of government in the United Kingdom and is prompting embarrassing questions about the disproportionate influence of such wealthy people.

The Arab Spring raised the issue of such inequities clearly in the minds of the poor and middle class. Protests like the Occupy Movement should serve as warnings of the limits of what restless populations are prepared to tolerate in democracies.

The fact that *Time* magazine chose the protesters as the person of the year for 2011 highlighted current frustration about inequities:

> All over the world, the protesters of 2011 shared a belief that their countries' political systems and economies have grown dysfunctional by corruption—sham democracies rigged to favor the rich and powerful and prevent significant change . . . they believe they're experiencing the failure of hell-bent megascaled crony hypercapitalism and pine for some third way, a new social contract.[6]

It may not take much more "let them eat cake-like" behavior to spawn a global form of the French Revolution aimed at toppling new-wealth aristocrats and targeting governments who support such inequities. One case of a local government being toppled due to unrest occurred in the spring of 2012 in the province of Quebec, Canada, when a student protest movement against tuition hikes morphed into a standoff over that society's future. The protest subsequently attracted many members of the disgruntled middle class, who connected "a number of the threads from environment and the state of public services to abuses in the financial industry over the past decade"[7] and established a street movement that toppled the provincial government and led to an election.

Further, after the widespread United Kingdom riots in 2011, Justice Secretary Ken Clarke may have had his finger on the real pulse of a growing segment of society when he referred to the rioters as representative of a "feral underclass"—pockets of society "cut off from the mainstream in everything but its materialism."[8] This expression was used presumably because the rioters resembled wild animals just released from captivity bent on destroying what they felt was harming them with no sense of a shared interest in the current form of society. Many of these people were poor and felt rejected and abandoned by society, being forced to live outside its institutions. While violence can almost never be condoned, who can blame people who have reached their breaking point and feel they have no voice or control over their destinies? As Ken Clarke pointed out, society needs to address "the appalling social deficits that the riots have highlighted."[9]

As well, anyone with common sense can see how unstable the current economic model is when, for example, it should be clear that most developed countries will never pay off burgeoning interest payments. The fact that the slightest economic news causes markets to stampede wildly from one direction to another is an indication that something is amiss. For the sake of stability, it is to some extent important to maintain the fiction of business as usual, but this becomes much more difficult when, as is occurring now, we are approaching the limits of this model.

At the same time, we need to be extremely careful in seeking to change the model to protect economic recovery and employment. In seeking a new economic model for society, it is important to promote those aspects of the current situation that continue to produce excellent results, such as entrepreneurial competition and efficient production and distribution of goods. As well, to minimize the fear that inevitably comes with change, adjustments might be made over a comfortable period of time to allow gradual adaptation to the more sustainable model. Unquestionably, however, some reform is necessary. If an unsustainable consumption-focused economic model can be invented, it can also be uninvented. America, which has taken the lead in creating so much social and economic innovation in the past, needs to draw on its deep well of reserves to promote the dialog required for a brave new sustainable economic model that takes into account the innate social and spiritual nature of people. We need a wiser and clearer vision of policymaking, a redefined social contract and economic model, and new notions of what comprises prosperity and wealth. Such a change must begin with the awareness of the following:

- the consequences of Charles Darwin's maxim that it is the most adaptable who survive;
- the fact that that beyond providing for basic needs, happiness and well-being do not come from consuming material goods;
- the unsustainable situation we are in and how the current economic model impacts us socially and spiritually;
- the need for a reevaluation of the material possessions actually needed and contemplation about how we might consume less;
- how we can reuse and recycle more;
- how we can seek well-being outside the conventional trappings of affluence, such as within relationships, family, and community;
- the long-term consequences on our children and grandchildren of not altering our habits, economic model, and course as a society; and
- the desirability of providing incentives and positive widespread recognition for individuals and corporations who practice high standards of ethics and social responsibility, and who take measures to minimize their ecological footprint.

At the government and public level, we ought to follow the following ten commandments:

TEN COMMANDMENTS FOR REFORM

1. To acknowledge that we live in a holistic reality, that our economic system must reflect this, and that we are on an unsustainable path resulting from the current economic model.

2. To understand that wealth and prosperity include social and spiritual returns and environmental sustainability.

3. To shift to a new economic model that creates its money supply without the debt-interest perils of having banks do this, possibly taking a restrictive approach to usury.

4. To introduce a new way of measuring the well-being of economies that rates them on sustainability efficiencies.

5. To include in addition to the kinds of social and spiritual returns mentioned on page 117 also an index of self-responsibility and self-reliance since people are happiest when providing for themselves.

6. To reorganize corporations into smaller units to avoid the "too big to fail" scenario experienced during the Great Recession of 2008—perhaps along the lines of Germany's "lean and efficient" family corporations, which, in certain circumstances, can be brought under a single mantle so that they can cooperate as if they were a large corporation to achieve specific objectives.

7. To continue to promote investment in lasting assets such as clean low-carbon technologies, good quality housing, efficient transport systems, public buildings, and open spaces.

8. To overhaul capital markets and their institutions to avoid the kind of unrestrained speculation in currencies, commodities, and financial derivatives that brought the financial system to the brink of collapse, including measures to instill higher morality into the system.

9. To encourage corporations through tax incentives and public recognition supported by forward-looking public policy to: (a) create more durable and easily recyclable products; (b) have carbon-efficient operations; and (c) utilize new social enterprises, such as B-corporations, which use the power of business to solve social and environmental problems.

10. To understand that when we have the data and knowledge to realize that the business-as-usual mind-set may seriously harm or even destroy the survival of our species, it is time for a new generation of enlightened leaders who understand the issues to inspire and implement.

A revolutionary strategy for transitioning to a richer, more creative life during a time of ecological and economic crisis is offered by Professor Juliet B. Schor in her book *Plenitude*.[10] Drawing on recent developments in economic theory, social analysis, and ecological design, she argues that through a major shift to new sources of wealth, green technologies, and different ways of living, individuals and nations can be better off and more economically secure. Schor contends that we must and can use fixed resources with greater efficiency, harnessing technology for productivity increases and enhanced human capital.[11] Individuals and governments need to spend more time pondering such essential ideas with a mind to creating a practical way forward to a more sustainable future. Our social and spiritual well-being depend on it in the short term, and our very long-term survival hinges on taking action *now*.

Chapter 18

FINDING COMMON GROUND

*There is nothing new under the sun, but there
are lots of old things we don't know.*

—AMBROSE BIERCE

While lots of new gadgetry in the digital age can be found, the fundamental nature of people has not changed, and we continue to make the same mistakes and lose sight of the "old things we don't know."

In contrast to our incremental social evolution, we are now facing rapidly growing technological change, which represents an astonishing and stress-inducing transformation. If we were to plot the rate of social versus technological evolution of the last 100 years on a graph, it might look something like figure 23. The fact is that people as social animals adapt very slowly while developing technology at an exponential rate.

Rate of Change

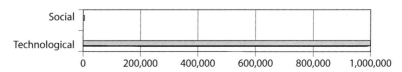

FIGURE 23   *The Pace of Social Versus Technological Change*

Our current economic model, including technological advances, is so out of sync with human social evolution that it should not be surprising that people feel so much social alienation and spiritual disconnection. As Marshall McLuhan suggested, we need to exercise greater prudence when the *medium is the message*, particularly when we don't know what the ultimate impacts of technology might be.

We need to collectively exercise our greatest strength as Homo sapiens and decide on a course of adaptation. To proceed forward, however, instead of focusing on what we perceive to be our differences, it is imperative that we acknowledge the common ground that binds us together as a species. We must all deal with the physical reality of existence on this tiny planet within a colossal cosmos—an actuality that we are only just beginning to understand. As a species, we have learned a lot in our short existence, but we are just now getting our first inkling of wisdom about what our sustainable role in nature should be. If we are adaptable and prudent, maybe we can extend our 12 hours of galactic existence to at least the 161 days of dinosaurs on earth.

As a species, we all share a common humanity that is hardwired into our social DNA. It is believed that Homo sapiens transitioned from Homo erectus—an extinct apelike species of humans regarded as our ancestor—only 300,000 to 400,000 years ago. In evolutionary terms, this is a mere eyeblink in time. It should not be surprising, then, as pointed out in *The Economic Dependency Trap*, that when people are put into the same circumstances, regardless of social or economic standing, ethnicity, or geographical location, they react similarly. From this perspective, the languages, cultures, religions, and views that have evolved from time immemorial are simply the lenses that color the views of a particular group—the underlying physical reality remains unchanged, regardless of who we are and what we choose to believe. At the end of the day, if we have created a civilization where people live in misery or that leads to destroying the planet, the differences that divide us will seem trifling.

In seeking common ground, we must also recognize that although people tend to see themselves as separate from everything else, we are simply a minuscule organic part of the cosmos. In addition, we must realize that we live in a complex universe where the one constant is change and acknowledge that the nature of the universe is the reality of all people and all species from time immemorial.

Although many individuals raised in a society where people have an intolerant religious, spiritual, scientific, or ethnic mind-set might have difficulty grasping that their accustomed way of thinking about social reality is just one possible viewpoint that has arisen at a specific moment in history because of a particular culture, language, religion, or geographical area, in an objective cosmic sense, there really are no "chosen people." Rather, we are all chosen people who have to deal with the same reality. We have a choice about whether we live our lives so as to embrace our families, communities, and healthy differences. We have the free will to make decisions to perpetuate a society that encompasses the fundamental qualities that make us human and allow us to adapt for our long-term survival. His Holiness the Dalai Lama has aptly commented, ". . . the more I see of the world, the clearer it becomes that no matter what our situation, whether we are rich or poor, educated or not, of one race, gender, religion or another, we all desire to be happy and to avoid suffering."[1] As long as the views of one group are not harming another, we should tolerate others in the spirit of respect, cooperation, and goodwill, recognizing that we are not diminished by differences as a species but are ultimately strengthened by them. Instead of promoting hate and suspicion about each other, we need to promote tolerance and understanding. We should celebrate the fact that in our differences lie great strength. At the same time, recognizing our common humanity, we should also seek to adopt those attitudes needed to build a better, more sustainable future to provide for our children and future generations.

Chapter 19

EMBRACING OUR PRIMAL NATURE

Deviation from nature is deviation from happiness.

—SAMUEL JOHNSON

*W*hat has been forgotten or ignored in our scramble for material riches is that people are social and spiritual creatures who need to nourish these innate aspects to be happy. We must actively seek to maintain a child's wonder about our existence and our place in the cosmos and embrace spiritual pursuits. Besides our spiritual practices and our interactions with others, one of the primary ways of doing this is to connect closely to the environment to reaffirm our own primal nature.

Although science, technology, and the culture of materialism have brought many benefits, unfortunately, they have combined to increase our isolation from social and physical environments. The result has been that some of the intuitive senses essential for our survival and our spiritual and social well-being have become diminished or lost.

As biological organisms with spiritual dimensions who have evolved from the animal kingdom, we are now losing our intuitive abilities, such as sensing danger or connecting to other nonhuman creatures. Originally, we had a powerful so-called sixth sense like many animals still do. For example, dogs can hear and sense danger and the presence of other life at great distances. Horses get spooked when something is not right and have been scientifically shown to pick up on the anxiety of their riders.[1] During the great 2004 tsunami in the Indian Ocean, despite the fact there were more than 230,000 people killed, there were virtually no animal casualties, due, presumably, to the fact that they sensed the impending danger and retreated to higher ground.[2] Even small children often exhibit a strong intuitive sense and are able to detect many imperceptible things that adults cannot. Unfortunately, as we age, society, through its institutions and technology, standardizes our perceptions and "civilizes" us in a way that diminishes our intuitive abilities and our connection with our spiritual dimension. Spending a great deal of time in artificial environments and focusing excessively on new technology and media also blind us to our primal nature, causing us to believe we are above such "animal" tendencies and reject the notion that we might be connected to nature in a way that gives us useful powers.

As we lose intuitive understanding, empathy, and a perception of ourselves as social and spiritual beings, we tend to be cavalier, destructive, and alienated, forgetting the important reasons that underlie such traits and values. However, instead of running roughshod over our primal nature, we should seek to understand how we are losing it, the potential consequences of this, and take intelligent, corrective measures where possible.

CONNECTING TO OTHER SPECIES

We need another and a wiser and perhaps a more mystical concept of animals . . . In a world older and more complete than ours they move finished and complete, gifted with extensions of the senses we have lost or never attained, living by voices we shall never hear. They are not brethren, they are not underlings; they are other nations, caught with ourselves in the net of life and time, fellow prisoners of the splendour and travail of the earth.

—HENRY BESTON

To embrace and nourish our primal nature and to obtain useful information for creating greater harmony in our daily lives, we can learn from groups that still have an intimate connection to nature and other creatures, such as my Native American community and other Native American communities. An example of such a connection with nature in my tribe occurred when my father, who was a chief of the Gitlan tribe, whose primary crest or protector totem is the wolf, or *laxgibuu* in the Tsimshian language, was in the final stage of stomach cancer. At noon, as medical personnel were moving him to the awaiting medevac helicopter to be flown from our tiny village to a hospital in a small city nearby, a loud chorus of howling wolves erupted near his house. While people in the community were accustomed to hearing wolves in the late evening or early morning, they never heard howling during the day.

Moreover, as if to reiterate the point, the wolves underscored the connection again the day after my father was laid to rest in a local community graveyard. Grave diggers in the cemetery who were preparing a new grave beside my father's burial plot were frightened away from their duties by wolves who came out of the woods to the graveside, exhibiting aggressive behavior that is out of character since wolves are generally shy around people. Even for Native Americans, such behavior honoring the ancient connection between the Gitlan and *laxgibuu* was surprising. What is not surprising to people of my tribe, however, is that such a bond between animals and people can and does exist if people are attuned to it.

Another astonishing example of such a bond between animals and humans was documented in Eden, Australia—in this instance between whales and humans. Because of a personal association with certain types of whales, one night I watched a fascinating documentary called *Killers in Eden*.[3] Tsimshian, like most tribes of the Canadian northwest coast, are matrilineal—meaning that family identity is connected through the mother's, not the father's, lineage as is common for Europeans—I belong to my mother's tribe, the Gitangangeek, whose primary crest or protector totem is the killer whale, referred to in the wild as *neext* in the Tsimshian language. Further, referred to as the "wolves of the sea" by Native Americans since they are very family-oriented, extraordinarily intelligent, and sensitive, these creatures have complex forms of communication and cooperate in hunts to an astonishingly sophisticated degree. For thousands of years, *neext* have hunted the great baleen whales.[4]

The Royal Helins Connected to Nature
(Author's father, *Sm'ooygit Nees Nuugan Noos* (Chief Barry Helin), with mother,
Sigyidm hana'a Su Dalx (Princess Verna Helin), wearing regalia and their crest
of wolf and orca, respectively.)

Although they are much smaller than baleen whales, their hunting technique is to drive them into shallow waters and drown them by taking turns breaching and landing on them when the baleen surface for air. In the open ocean, *neext* cannot follow the baleen sounding to great ocean depths so it is necessary to have a well-honed strategy working in close synchronization as a pack.

Other than unrecorded instances of the long history of indigenous tribes with whales,[5] this is the only recorded instance documented of *neext* cooperating with humans to hunt other whales. The film discussed, upon returning from rich feeding grounds in Antarctica to their breeding grounds on Australia's east coast, baleen whales pass within the vicinity of Twofold Bay, where the town of Eden is located. Since the waters there are shallower, *neext* learned this was a good place to wait for them, as did Europeans when they arrived in the area.

It was in this location that three generations of whalers from the non-indigenous Davidson family connected to *neext*.[6] *Neext* would drive baleen whales into the shallow waters, where members of the Davidson family would harpoon them. The family had an unspoken agreement with the *neext*, known to the family as the "law of the tongue," whereby the Davidsons would leave the dead baleen whales in the bay overnight before processing them, so the *neext* could take their tongues and lips, encouraging the *neext* to drive baleen whales to the location again in the future. This process made it much safer and easier for the whalers to catch the whales and led to far less waste than if *neext* hunted alone.

The Davidson family was also often invited by *neext* to go out to sea to join in their hunts. A few members of a pod of *neext* would swim near the Davidsons' houses and on murky nights breach or thrash their tails on the water surface until the whalers rowed out to meet them, following the bioluminescent trails created by the wakes of *neext*.

Further, the relationship between the Davidsons and the *neext* was so close that the whalers would even rescue *neext* if they became entangled in lines and nets, and the *neext* would, in turn, protect the Davidsons

Neext Hunts

from sharks or drowning if their small whaling boats were struck by the massive thrashing tails of baleen whales and shattered. This relationship was documented for over a hundred years in media reports, police records, court transcripts, diaries, postcards, government Hansard records, books, and tape and video oral history accounts.[7] Despite the skepticism of scientists and people from a technological world alienated from nature and unattuned to such connections with animals, the Davidsons and the people of Eden clearly understood this symbiotic relationship with *neext*. Similarly, from time immemorial, indigenous people have acknowledged and respected such a connection with other animals.

What modern people have forgotten is that they remain part of it and still have the ability to connect with nature in such ways. They also do not realize that when they destroy other life-forms, they destroy their spiritual brothers and sisters. It is in acknowledgment of this relationship that indigenous people traditionally showed gratitude and respect when they took animals for sustenance. Our economic and ecological path forward should be based on a similar understanding of and respect for nature and animals.

RELATING TO OUR SPIRITUAL DIMENSION

A knowledge of the existence of something we cannot penetrate, of the manifestations of the profoundest reason and the most radiant beauty— it is this knowledge and this emotion that constitute the truly religious attitude; in this sense, and in this alone, I am a deeply religious man.

—ALBERT EINSTEIN

In today's technological world, people are skeptical about the inherent social and spiritual nature of humans. But we need to acknowledge this truth: people are social and spiritual beings. This understanding should be at the heart of everything we undertake, as well as the institutions we create. Rather than ignoring our intrinsic spiritual nature, we should seek to comprehend how we are losing it, the potential consequences of this, and how we can take corrective measures to support it within the institutions we live by. If our economic model eventually leads to financial bankruptcy, our position will be immeasurably exacerbated if we are also socially and spiritually insolvent—losing the greatest sources of human strength and comfort in the face of adversity.

Chapter 20

THE PLACE OF THE TRIBE IN AN ANONYMOUS WORLD

Call it a clan, call it a network, call it a family. Whatever you call it, whoever you are, you need one.

—JANE HOWARD

*T*hough modern society has long since moved from basic tribal and community social organization to organization of greater scale and complexity, people still have an innate communal tendency and instinctive desire for tribal associations. David Berreby, an award-winning science writer, noted in his book *Us and Them: Understanding Your Tribal Mind,* "Homo sapiens is inescapably a tribal animal."[1]

Similarly, in his book *Social Intelligence,*[2] psychologist Daniel Goleman, Ph.D., explains how we are "wired to connect" and that since we are designed for sociability, when we gather, we instinctively engage in a "neural ballet" connecting brain to brain with those around us.[3] This is evidence of our innate communal tendency and tribal nature in addition to our need for individual expression.

UNDERSTANDING THE TRIBAL MAP

Further, according to Berreby, making tribal distinctions, or seeing the world in terms of *us and them,* comes from our minds through what he calls the "human-kind map." Humankind, he suggests, are tribal divisions that involve "hot cognition," those thoughts that cause, and are caused by, emotions and actions that make us act.[4] He also maintains that the human-kind map tells us what and who we are and determines our sense of well-being (*feeling* right) and morality. Our tribe, whether it is our family, ethnicity, religion, nation, or civic group, is made up of these feelings, as are the tribes we hate or think we hate.[5]

Berreby claims additionally that we have the power to decide how to use the tribal code and can control how we react when the code is invoked by others,[6] allowing us to make and remake our tribe. Berreby explains, "You could think of it as a set of buttons and levers built in to your mind. You didn't choose the control panel, but you can decide how to live with it. Push your own buttons and pull your own levers . . . Human kinds [tribal divisions] exist because of the human mind. They're in your head, bound to your fears and hopes, your sweat glands and your gut. But how you choose to live with them is up to you."[7]

HARDWIRED FOR THE TRIBE

Nobody has ever before asked the nuclear family to live all by itself in a box the way we do. With no relatives, no support, we've put it in an impossible situation.

—MARGARET MEAD

While we clearly cannot go back to a time of early tribal social organization, and we certainly do not want to endorse the destructive tribal infighting that has led to ethnic cleansing in nations throughout the world, there is an extremely valuable upside to tribal life that should be recognized and nurtured within contemporary society. Unlike some solitary species preferring to live alone, people are social animals who have learned that forming tribes has many social benefits, including opportunities for the sharing of work and pleasure, providing better defenses of groups, giving members a sense of belonging to a larger social unit that may take care of them when times are tough, and underscoring the interdependent nature of human existence.

In social psychology, the need to belong is considered a motivation for affiliating with others and being socially accepted.[8] And psychologist

Abraham Maslow has suggested that the need to belong is a basic source of human motivation more powerful than the desire for esteem or for self-actualization.

THE IMPORTANCE OF BELONGING

The hunger to belong is not merely the desire to be attached to something. It is rather sensing that great transformation and discovery become possible when belonging is sheltered and true.

—JOHN O'DONOHUE

Having a sense of belonging has great importance for our self-esteem, sense of well-being, and feeling of safety—as I have experienced during various phases of my life. Though I was brought up in a tribal culture, when I was 12 I was sent away from my family and remote little village community to a big city to get an education and was transplanted into the home of an upper-crust English family. Though the family members I lived with were wonderful, initially I found them to be formal and emotionally distant, rarely displaying emotion to the extent that was common in my Native American family.

What was familiar to me from my tribal family is characteristic of most Native American cultures, in which family and extended family are central and have a highly developed sense of interconnectedness, what I call a warm and reassuring "emotional community." Typically, family and tribal members demonstrate their affection openly through speech, gestures, and kind acts, making members feel intrinsically valuable and that they have a useful place. Perhaps there was such an emotional community in the English household, but I could not initially penetrate the veneer of formality to recognize it. Subsequently, I lived with a Chinese family, whose language and customs seemed even more perplexing to me.

As I matured, I eventually began to understand the value of having your cultural psyche stretched in such a way while you are young. I now feel very comfortable moving from culture to culture and have learned what a huge advantage it is for business and general life experience. However, at the time, my initial feeling I was losing my tribe was a frightening and painful experience that undermined my self-confidence. The longer I was away from my tribal culture, the more alienated I felt when I returned home. Though I did not realize it at the time, I was unwittingly becoming an outsider to my indigenous tribe. At the same time, I also did not seem to fit in my new urban culture. I felt as though I had been marooned alone on a remote island and was desperately homesick for the comfortable tribal sense of belonging I had experienced as a child. However, as I grew older, I eventually reconciled my original tribal life with the life I had subsequently developed while studying and living with families of other ethnicities in a city. I began to see how combining the strengths of my tribal heritage with aspects of the new cultures and networks to which I had been exposed was advantageous for my roles as businessperson, attorney, and writer, and gave me an even greater source of strength. I also began to understand how the alienation, pain, and loneliness I had experienced as an adolescent was a widespread phenomenon in the anonymous and disconnected existence of modern life.

Scientific research is now confirming that the sense of belonging to a tribe—the feeling of we or us as opposed to them—is extremely important for maintaining a balanced life and a sense of well-being. David Berreby noted that "we-feeling" is good for our health, lowering the heart rate, reducing stress hormones, making us sleep better and think more clearly. On the other hand, "them-feeling"—the self-perception that we are not recognized as part of the human community—is bad for us, resulting in jumbled thinking, anger, sadness, and a shorter life span. He concludes that an innate preference for "we-feeling" rather than "them-feeling" is no sideshow but one of life's main events.[9]

Losing the tribe is not just a problem of poor people in ghettoes, some of whom join gangs to feel they belong somewhere, but is a rapidly increasing problem impacting all strata of society. From 1950 to 1994, the number of households with only one person increased from 10 percent to 24 percent[10] and was 28 percent by 2012.[11] Incredibly, statistics further suggest that people who are isolated and healthy are twice as likely to die over a period of a decade as those not isolated.[12] As a result, a study comparing data from 1985 and 2004 found that the number of people with whom Americans can discuss matters important to them dropped by nearly one-third, from 2.94 people in 1985 to 2.08.[13]

While being alone is not the same thing as experiencing loneliness and disconnectedness, distressful feelings of isolation that come from not being part of a group or social network are also becoming increasingly prevalent in America. One major study by a leading scholar found that 60 million people in America are unhappy because of loneliness.[14] Further, those who experience loneliness tend to distance themselves from such uncomfortable feelings, instead, seeking comfort in unhealthy distractions such as alcohol or drugs, overeating, gambling, or watching too much television.[15] As well, loneliness increases the likelihood of being put in a geriatric home at an earlier age; exercising less, and becoming more obese; not surviving a major operation; hormonal imbalances; poor memory; depression; poor sleep; dementia; and general cognitive decline.[16]

Increasing social isolation, and related factors, has led to a rise in the numbers of various kinds of caregivers, which have increased from 33,000 in 1940 to 534,000 in 2010, as seen in figure 24.[17] The result is that what used to be only a matter of public concern about societal disintegration has become a matter of public health management. These changes may be partly due to the fact that since the modern economy requires great mobility, many people must move away from their communities and social support networks such as friends and family. As a result, countless people have become like plankton, floating in the vast sea of anonymity, and are frequently unable to fulfill their need for tribal belonging.

If people as social animals derive their greatest happiness and sense of purpose from their close social relations, unfortunately, this cannot be

Year	Clinical Psychologists	Clinical Social Workers	Non-Clinical Social Workers	Marriage Counselors & Family Therapists	Mental Health Counselors	Substance Abuse Counselors
1940s	2,500	30,000		500		
2010	177,000	192,000	400,000	50,000	105,000	220,000

FIGURE 24 *Increase in Caregivers Due (in part) to Social Isolation*

done in a society where individuals are becoming increasingly isolated from other people.

CREATING THE NEO-TRIBE

Positive feelings come from being honest about yourself and accepting your personality, and physical characteristics, warts and all; and, from belonging to a family that accepts you without question.

—WILLARD SCOTT

Gaining an awareness of people's increasing social alienation and spiritual disconnection in today's society and its harmful impacts can help us understand what we need and how we can reestablish some sense of tribal connection, which is critically important for our well-being. We must, however, accommodate our need for tribal connection in a way that can be adapted to the circumstances of the modern world. Once we recognize that we are on a course that is harming our social and spiritual well-being, we have the power to consciously choose a path that is healthier and more fulfilling by intentionally creating our own new tribe, one that suits our character and lifestyle. We can understand how this can be done by examining some tribal structures.

A typical example of tribal organization is that of the Maori of Aotearoa (New Zealand), illustrated in figure 25.[18] The individual is the basic unit of the tribe, and social connections extend outward to the family (*whanua*), subtribe (*hapu*), and tribe (*iwi*). But the neo-tribe does not have to have the same structure to be beneficial.

In my life, I have unwittingly created various levels of tribal connection which essentially make up my neo-tribe. At the core of my tribe are my immediate and extended family by actual kinship. Then there is my extended tribe as the result of what I call "Indian adoption." Traditionally, in Native American communities, when a family could not look after one of their offspring, another family or community member took the child

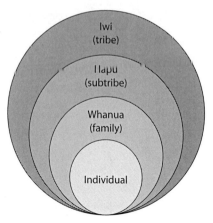

FIGURE 25 *Tribal Organization of the Maori of New Zealand*

or children, with the agreement of the parents, and raised them as their own. I had the privilege of creating extended tribal connections with the families who looked after me in the city where I was forced to move as an adolescent. I also consciously expanded my neo-tribe by creating close friendships with good people I met at various stages in my life.

The next level of my neo-tribe is comprised of people with whom I spend a lot of my time and for whom I have developed familylike fondness. Such a group consists of children and underprivileged students in the inner-city karate club where I have taught for the last 11 years, many of whom have literally grown up in the club. In some respects, contributing to the growth and development of young people is an enormous reward in itself, evoking, at times, feelings akin to being a proud parent.

This example underscores an important aspect of creating our own neo-tribe—giving. It is a cosmic truth that the more we selflessly give, the more the universe returns to us. Giving with our heart and purest intentions to individuals or organizations in dire need is a wonderfully rewarding way to create our neo-tribe. When we give our time to organizations in ways like volunteering at food banks or working with kids as coaches, mentors, or instructors, we immediately expand our neo-tribe to include people who share similar values and are likely to be supportive.

The next level in my neo-tribe consists of my real Native American tribe, apart from my immediate family. Since I have not lived in the area where my real tribe is located for most of my life, my actual tribal connections are not as strong as some I have created with my neo-tribe throughout my life.

The final level of my neo-tribe is comprised of people with whom I have socialized and gotten to know well over a long period of time, such as my Friday night soccer buddies, close associates in educational and other fields, and people with whom I have served on various boards.

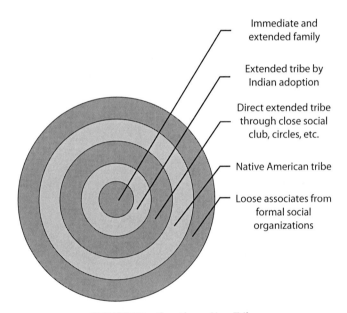

Immediate and extended family

Extended tribe by Indian adoption

Direct extended tribe through close social club, circles, etc.

Native American tribe

Loose associates from formal social organizations

FIGURE 26 *Creating a Neo-Tribe*

In seeking to create or expand our neo-tribe, we should keep in mind the following points: (1) We all need the social and sometimes physical contact that comes from having one; (2) the healthier our neo-tribe, the healthier we will be; and (3) there is no formula for creating one. As everyone takes their own path in life, we all have our own method of creating a neo-tribe; knowing the importance of having a tribe and the perils of not having one in the modern world of broken relations, fractured families, and single-person households should motivate us. Consequently, *Wai wah!* or "Just do it!" in the Tsimshian language.

Chapter 21

FINDING COMMUNITY IN THE URBAN DESERT

The good we secure for ourselves is precarious and uncertain until it is secured for all of us and incorporated into our common life.

—JANE ADDAMS

*L*ike belonging to a tribe, feeling part of a community helps diminish isolation and disconnection. While notions of being part of a community and belonging to a tribe overlap, there are some critical differences. The kinds of people who make up our tribe in the contemporary world are largely chosen by us, while the individuals in our community come from a broader base. For example, our tribe may consist of family and close friends, but our community can be comprised of a range of people of varying social backgrounds, races, and religions with whom we interact in society on a daily or weekly basis. In many respects, our community reflects the kind of person we are.

Being part of a community has many benefits, including the sharing of work and knowledge, increased social interaction, support, and cooperation. The phrase "It takes a village to raise a child," expressed in the Nigerian Igbo proverb as *Ora na azu nwa*,[1] underscores the value of community for sharing skill sets and cooperation. By contrast, a problem with the nuclear families of the Western world is that members often participate in activities and raise their children largely alone, which is not only exhausting but often cuts them off from the larger community. But, it makes no sense for people to be isolated from the greatest source of social nourishment that can be essential for psychic health. I know from personal experience that being brought up in a large and stable family is one of the greatest gifts that we can be given in life. My family home was always filled with close relatives, laughter, and lessons involving responsibility, learning to compromise, and other valuable social skills needed to interact in a good way with other people. There really is no other good way to raise children; replacing communities and families with money and government programs simply creates false social and financial expectations that a government and its agencies can never fulfill in the future.

Communities exist for the same reason that wolf packs and orca pods do: because people are social beings who value interaction, cooperation, and sharing labor and experiences. We have an inherent understanding that the greatest benefits and most rewarding things in life come from interacting cooperatively with other people and that a sense of community is important for establishing peace and harmony in society.

A recent study from *Proceedings of Royal Society B*, a journal published by Britain's academy of sciences, even states that working cooperatively leads to bigger human brain size, as growth is spurred through social interaction.[2] The study also suggests that cooperation occurs because people recognize the importance of reciprocity and self-interest since they realize that cooperation with others in the present will likely result in receiving help in the future. In fact, the primary survival advantage people have over other species is our inherently social nature, which is expressed cooperatively through our families and communities.

I was raised in a remote Native American community that consisted of nine distinct tribes. Prior to the flood of government funding, people worked collectively with an unspoken understanding of the importance of reciprocity to self-interest. For example, when my grandmother needed a house, community members milled the wood and built the house, knowing that this would be reciprocated when their elders were in need—and it was. The community also built two sports clubs with gyms, where families volunteered their time and services to organize a variety of sporting and social events that bonded members of the community. I have vivid and fond memories of my uncles and aunts visiting, playing cards, having parties, as well as attending sporting and community social events. Such communal cooperation and interaction led to social cohesion and a healthy social environment characterized by mutual respect.

Unfortunately, however, this strong sense of community largely ended with the deluge of government social welfare dollars and the myth that the government was going to take care of everyone, as was documented in my book *Dances with Dependency*. Once it was clear that people did not need to rely on each other for their sustenance, community cohesion and mutual respect were replaced by lateral violence, learned helplessness, and some of the most alarming social pathologies in the developed world today. As is happening in mainstream society, drugs and alcohol are filling the cracks that have opened due to a lack of social interaction.

Governments can only provide a little money for sustenance but can never replace the social fabric of communities or of tribal networks, nor create the irreplaceable social skills and knowledge that have evolved from millennia of cooperative experience. The fact remains that people have to, and will always need to, look after one another through their own network of close social relations.

While some modern-day forms of communities may fulfill some functions of traditional communities, they can also have drawbacks. When I was introduced to one commune—an intentional community of people who had agreed to live together, sharing common interests, property, and possessions—its limitations became evident. Theoretically, it was a good idea and was led by a brilliant intellectual and leading thinker on the value and theory of communities, philosopher and Professor Fred Brown. In practice, however, it seemed to consist of a group of effete and self-righteous intellectuals who were only marginally committed to the idea of hard work or self-sacrifice. Big talk of grand dreams without action led to third-world living conditions. About the only item that stirred any interest or resulted in work was maintaining the communal marijuana patch whose fruits were the topic of constant discussion and frequent sampling.

Today, there is much buzz about the "communities" created by social media such as Facebook and Twitter. Though such social media provide an opportunity to establish a kind of virtual association, I don't regard such virtual associations as real communities, as they do not involve real communities, a sense of responsibility or obligation that accompanies the myriad invaluable benefits of real communities. They are simply a convenient communications tool linking a broad network of people with shallow connections.

The depth of community that can be created from sitting in front of a computer is minimal, although such social media may reinforce real face-to-face communities and their activities. Surrogate alternatives of connection can never replace the critical social bonds of which healthy communities consist.

One of the world's leading experts on loneliness, John Cacioppo, the author of the 2008 book *Loneliness*, notes that the idea that a Web site can deliver a friendlier interconnected world is bogus because it is the depth of one's social network outside of social media like Facebook that determines the depth of one's connections within it—not the other way around.[3] In other words, the strength of connections generated in the real face-to-face world of real communities is what results in real-world communities, not a loose affiliation of acquaintances over a communications device. Stephen Marche in his article in *The Atlantic* titled "Is Facebook Making Us Lonely?" arrived at essentially the same conclusion that might be summarized as: Internet social networking simply creates a communications connection and not the authentic social bond that can be found in real communities.[4]

By contrast, real communities that are the basis of societal relationships require face-to-face commitment and constant effort. The thoughtful visits, phone calls, family dinners, parties, or other social events that someone takes the care and time to organize are what bolster social cohesion. If a strong community is desired, everyone in it needs to understand its value and be prepared to do the things necessary to reinforce close social relations. Rather than support a sense of community among people, to-day's social networking arguably actually undermines the communal fabric of real society.

Consequently, we should cultivate our real communities consisting of our families, friends, neighbors, school or work associates, sporting teams and other activity groups, and social clubs. We should all make an ongoing commitment and effort to be friendly and engaged with neighbors, to coach children's teams, volunteer at the food bank, or to join the local soccer team or business club. Such actions are the fabric of what it means to belong to a real community. We should understand the effort that is needed to create and maintain such relations and recognize that the rewards are well-balanced people and a healthy society.

When everything is said and done, having real communities is vital to the well-being of people. Apart from all the other benefits of communities, ultimately, we need them because to become the people we hope to be we must raise our children in healthy social environments where they can learn the social skills and character traits required to survive and get on well in life. Communities help us express the essence of what it means to be social animals and allow us to share the gift of our consciousness with others. Unless we evolve into something entirely different from what we are, the need for communities will always be a characteristic of the human social animal.

Chapter 22

THE IMPORTANCE OF MYTH, RITUAL, AND CEREMONY

Myths are public dreams, dreams are private myths.

—JOSEPH CAMPBELL

While myths, rituals, and ceremonies formed the foundation of philosophies, religions, and cultures of many past societies, they continue to have value for people in today's societies, who often feel anonymous, alienated from society, and disconnected from their spiritual dimension. For this discussion, the exact nature of the relationship between myth, ritual, and ceremony is not important but rather the value they continue to have for people in society who feel adrift in the anonymous sea that is modern life.

In addition to old myths in our current society, there is the new mythos espousing unbridled consumption and economic growth that is impacting our cultural mind-set and having unfortunate repercussions that are not fully understood because they are clothed in revered science and rationality. This chapter will look at the fundamentally important reasons for placing a high value on such practices and the importance of myth, ritual, and ceremony in modern life.

THE POWER AND PLACE OF MYTH

Since the nature of people is bad, to become corrected they must be taught a new mythology by teachers and to be orderly they must acquire ritual and moral principles.

—XUN ZI

Myths are traditional stories or legends, usually concerning some being, hero, heroine, or courageous event, and may involve deities or demigods

149

who explain some practice, rite, or phenomenon of nature.[1] Myths, which are largely shaped by the environment, are thought to explain how things came to be, to teach lessons or values, unify a group or define a group's identity, explain social or religious rituals, or provide entertainment.

Historically, according to Joseph Campbell,[2] artists were the myth-makers from whom ceremonies and rituals flowed. Myths arose from elite artists who were particularly gifted, "whose ears and eyes were open to the song of the universe."[3] In traditional cultures, however, shamans had this role. They were not magicians, as is thought in popular culture, but were much like priests whose teachings and powers were symbolized in deities of one's own personal experience. They typically were people who became shamans "as the result of intense psychological experiences that turned them inward so that their whole unconsciousness . . . opened up . . ."[4] The knowledge they acquired from such a state could include near-death experiences during which they returned from powerful dreams that connected them to the majesty of the spirit. In other cultures, priests and mystics practiced forms of meditation and ceremonies to transcend from the material world to the spiritual world.

In the contemporary context, the popular notion of myths is that they are relics of a bygone era when people needed simple stories to provide guidance and comfort in an uncertain world and that they have little relevance in modern life. For example, Native American myths about the creation of the world, which often invoke supernatural beings and surrealistic events, are often viewed today as charming stories from more primitive times. It is presumed that we now live in an era enlightened by reason, science, and technology with a vastly improved material culture and a superior understanding of nature and, therefore, do not need such antiquated and scientifically unverifiable stories.

What has been lost in the thinking that myths do not have an important function today is the fact that myths are generally not intended to be interpreted literally and that the fundamental aspects of human nature, and the cosmos which myths reflect, have not changed. The real importance of such stories is in the attitudes and values that they teach for the harmonious and long-term survival of people. According to Joseph Campbell in *Creative Mythology*, myths serve four functions, which can be seen as pertaining to the human condition in general and thus relevant today:

1. **Religious/Spiritual:** myths are meant to make people experience the powerful feeling of the divine in their lives.

2. **Cosmological:** myths serve to render a cosmology, an image of the universe which might include how things like time, space, and biology work and are organized—for example, how the world and its creatures came to be.

3. **Social:** myths maintain an established order where wisdom-rich models for social behavior convey their meaning through parables containing moral lessons which teach us how we should behave—the difference between model behavior and what is unacceptable.

4. **Psychological:** myths symbolize important points in an individual's life, with the purpose of centering and harmonizing the individual since such stories help us to look for life answers and guidance *within ourselves,* to understand *our own* narratives, and, with the help of their symbolism, tap into a valid source: one's *self,* which happens to contain all of the universe anyway.[5]

An example of "social" myths might be *Aesop's Fables,* where animal characters teach children folk wisdom to help them understand human nature and human behavior. "The Goose and the Golden Egg" teaches that those who have plenty and want more may lose what they already have by being too greedy, while "The Fox and the Monkey" provides the moral lesson that a true leader proves himself through his character. Modern people are largely blind to the fact that the views critically discussed in this book—concerning the supremacy of rational thinking and science, the superiority of Western culture, the paramount importance of the economic model and its requirement for constant growth, of consumption, money, and power—constitute the current mythos, which might be called "The Scientific and Economic Progress of Rational, Modern Humankind."

The economic and social values at the core of this current mythos would involve the following:

- People are not really part of the animal kingdom or nature, and since we are not connected to either, our impact on biodiversity or the environment does not matter.

- What is most important is that people take as much for themselves as quickly as possible, and it doesn't matter what tomorrow brings or whether we are on a sustainable path or not.

- Power, material possessions, and money are what count most. Nature's gifts of biodiversity and environment are simply available to be turned into money for people's benefit.

- The economic model, its growth imperative, and the money it delivers are the most important items to the well-being of society, while human social and spiritual needs are secondary.

- Those who seek to win at all costs, such as capitalists, entrepreneurs, bankers, and hedge fund managers, are the modern heroes, and the morality and social and spiritual of impacts of their actions do not matter.

Once we understand how this mythos shapes our cultural mind-set and social values, it becomes clear how we have ended up with an economic model that has created so much destruction and human misery. When the values underlying our mythos are so far out of sync with our natural place in the cosmos and inherent nature, the result is harmful—power, possessions, and money have neither conscience nor regard for the deeper social and spiritual interests of people. In comparison with the functions of myths outlined by Joseph Campbell, it is apparent that our modern mythos mostly serves to emphasize a materialistic cosmology and largely ignores the religious, spiritual, social, and psychological values that have always been central to a mythos of a society.

While we may have unwittingly created such a mythos over a long period of time, it is important to be aware of how it is currently impacting us. It is equally important to understand that we have the power to alter the mythos in a way that is more beneficial to our long-term interests. We must intentionally determine how to do this with a unified voice and stand together behind a wiser decision about our future.

A mythos that better supports the innate social and spiritual aspects of humans should incorporate the following ideas that reflect new priorities:

• People are intrinsically part of the animal kingdom and nature. Since they are so connected to the cosmos, their impact on biodiversity and the environment matters enormously.

• What is most important is that people take only what they need for themselves to live well, doing this with the understanding of how their actions affect the future counts. Since the resources of the world are finite, they should seek a sustainable course and leave a healthy legacy for future generations.

• People living in balance with nature and in harmonious relationships are what count most. The planet's biodiversity and environment are nature's gifts, and people should recognize their irreplaceable value and collectively share in their bounty in a way that creates the greatest harmony and provides for their needs as social and spiritual beings.

• The economic model and the money it delivers should serve the social and spiritual well-being of all in society in a sustainable manner, while accumulating material wealth, consumption, power, and money should be secondary.

• The heroes of modern mythology are those people who promote greater social and spiritual good for all in everything they do—morality and the social and spiritual impact of these heroes is of utmost importance.

We do not need to go back to the mythos that existed in the Dark Ages to encompass what people need now. Rather, we need to weave the scientific and other advances that currently exist into a reinvented mythos that leads to a more satisfying and sustainable way of life. Taking these advantageous ideas into account in creating a new mythos, we can adopt what is needed for a kinder, gentler, and more sustainable future guided by wisdom, rather than the simple wanton lust for material possessions.

THE VALUE OF RITUAL AND CEREMONY IN MODERN LIFE

A commercial society whose members are essentially ascetic and indifferent in social ritual has to be provided with blueprints and specifications for evoking the right tone for every occasion.

—MARSHALL MCLUHAN

A *ritual* is defined as "a religious or solemn ceremony consisting of a series of actions performed according to a prescribed order."[6] A *ceremony* is a more formal act or series of acts prescribed by ritual, protocol, or convention,[7] usually with an important religious, spiritual, or conventional purpose, such as a marriage ceremony. In general, rituals and ceremonies serve to impose order on our chaotic lives and are often performed primarily for their symbolic value.

Ritual and ceremony can eliminate anxiety by providing a prescription for what to do or say in difficult situations—including the use of manners and attitudes of humility, respect, and appreciation for the worth of cooperation—values and knowledge that are disappearing in a narcissistic society but are beneficial in many ways. Manners, for example, lubricate everyday human relations and ensure that people feel they are being respectfully addressed or treated so that interactions between people occur smoothly. According to a Chinese proverb, "Ceremony is the smoke of friendship."[8] Further, use of ceremonial words can ensure a proper attitude of respect among people to promote learning of beneficial societal structures. In the past, for example, children were required to refer to adults and teachers by formal titles, a practice now considered old-fashioned in informal contemporary society. But we have forgotten that the real purpose for this was to promote an attitude of respect for older people or those in authority, which has important implications in today's world where respect for elders and authority figures is often lacking.

In karate, for example, students call their instructor *Sensei*, which means teacher or master. In Japanese, *Sensei* is someone who is your teacher, not your friend or equal, but is the person in a higher position with knowledge and the ability to teach you. Such an important relationship requires the proper mutual respect of roles to work effectively. Use of such language invokes a mind-set conducive to student learning.

Ancient Chinese philosopher Xun Zi summarized the value of ritual and teaching, saying, "A person should first be changed by a teacher's instructions, and guided by principles of ritual. Only then can he observe the rules of courtesy and humility, obey the conventions and rules of society, and achieve order."[9] Another example of how a ritual can provide a right attitude is in the ritual of prayer, which puts people in their proper place in the cosmos, often emphasizing humility, empathy, and kindness. When we pray, whatever our religion, spirituality, ethnicity, or beliefs, we are also closer to nature in a way that emphasizes our true insignificance in the greater universe.

Another benefit of ritual is that it can introduce elements of beauty or the sacred into everyday life that can be inspiring or underscore our connection with other beings and elements of the universe. Ceremony and ritual, according to Joseph Campbell, functions to take us out of our comfort zone to our inner spiritual reality, which is critical to our well-being and ensures we are in balance with the cosmos. Material things can never function in this way. In fact, as suggested in the Sermon on the Mount, the more we focus on material possessions, the further we become removed from the spiritual inner world. As biological creatures, we need food, water, and a place to live, but excess material possessions only serve to distract us from leading a more gratifying spiritual existence.

Use of ritual and ceremony are also the primary ways of promoting harmony and reducing friction in society. Losing our rituals and ceremonies means that we also lose deeper, more meaningful ways of connecting to each other. Philosopher and scholar Confucius considered the acts of everyday life to be rituals. Over 1,600 years ago, his writings articulated his belief that ritual served to unite people and strengthen the human community.

Additionally, ritual and ceremony also provide for the most important and fundamental requirement to live a happy and balanced life: self-identity. It is common for Native Americans to say, "We are our ceremonies, and our ceremonies are who we are." In 1893, the official report of the Bureau of Ethnology said, "The most surprising fact relating to North American Indians which until lately had not been realized is that they habitually lived in and by religion [expressed through their rituals and ceremonies] to a degree comparable to ancient Israelites under theocracy."[10] Important and often lengthy ceremonies were practiced throughout the year, which were reinforced by daily rituals whose purpose was to invoke the appropriate mind-set of humility, place in the cosmos, and care for people and the environment.

Once we understand how ceremonies are such an intrinsic part of Native American life, it becomes much easier to comprehend the notion that our ceremonies are us. No matter what group we belong to, if our rituals and ceremonies are taken away, we lose our identity. And if we do not know who we are, we will not know how to live or behave appropriately—the very foundation of a civilized society.

People have evolved from time immemorial with spiritual dimension hardwired into our DNA, and thus, the notion that we could replace such an important aspect of what it means to be a human being with the inadequate substitutes of the material world is unrealistic. Once we all understand this very fundamental proposition, we can begin to adapt in ways required for support of our spiritual and social needs—and not simply continue to pander to our weaknesses.

Ishi Prays for the World

CONCLUSION

易经

(Sinogram for the *I Ching*, which is literally translated as
"The Principle of Changes"[1])

Certain things may catch your eye,
But pursue only those
that capture your heart.

—ANCIENT NATIVE AMERICAN PROVERB

According to scholar Jung Young Lee, the wisdom of the *I Ching* (one of the Chinese classics) teaches that, "The greatness of Chinese mentality does not lie in its logical system of thought but in the intuitive insight derived directly from the nature of spiritual reality."[2] In truth, the greatness of any culture lies in how it uses intuitive insight to connect to the spirit for the purpose of creating the best attainable society. To do this, we need to understand the transformative nature of the cosmos so we may successfully adapt to change and the spiritual dimension of people so we can nourish it. When people have such a spiritual dimension etched into their DNA, it simply makes good sense to cultivate it. It also makes sense to have a clear vision of the dynamic nature of change and the adaptation required to ensure we survive intact.

Today, we urgently need to find our way to a wiser and more meaningful existence using ancient wisdom to cultivate more harmony, gentleness, and kindness in our lives. A society that ignores the spiritual dimension of its people sets itself on a course of needless confusion and unnecessary suffering. Such an imbalance is reflected in our modern society fraught with loneliness, growing anxiety, and a sense of purposelessness. Millions feel a crushing desperation, alienation, and lack of spiritual connection to a higher state of being or awareness. Many of those people comprehend the need for something more fulfilling in life but are unsure about what that might be.

Instead, we have created a society that has chosen the atomistic to the holistic, where rationality, consumption, and materialism trump long-neglected spiritual and social needs. This has led to massive inequities, where many feel they have no shared interest in a society. Unprecedented levels of stress, substance abuse, divorce and family breakups, homelessness, and incarceration attest to the rapidly devolving social disintegration. On the streets, frustration is reflected in social explosions like the Occupy Movement and the growing powder keg of dissatisfaction building in the middle class who increasingly feel the system is rigged for the privileged and wealthy.

In recent history, we have embraced a form of capitalism that has unquestionably delivered enormous benefits. However, as this economic model has evolved, its deficiencies have become clear—it is a system that has been on the ropes for some time and may be down for the count, if fundamental adjustments are not made soon. In earlier times, it might have been possible for industrialized Western nations to consume their way to prosperity. But, with unprecedented levels of personal and government debt, burgeoning population growth, and finite natural resources, this path is obviously not sustainable. It should also be clear that excessive consumption and materialism, on their own, are not likely to lead to social and spiritual well-being.

Enormous pressure has been placed on natural resources as the result of population growth and rapid industrialization of highly populated nations. We are witnessing for the first time in history the limits of an economic model that demands constant growth. Unless we reign in the economic horses, the social and spiritual cart is in danger of falling into the abyss with it.

The world is in desperate need of leadership and dialog about reforming the economic model which determines how we spend most of our conscious time. In marketing, the word *mindshare* means the amount of consumer awareness created for purposes of selling a particular product. Along this line, leaders need to "sell" a discourse about such reform so that there is a "collective mindshare" in society to build support for action leading to change in the self-interest of everyone.

We must be inventive and initiate a system that has less impact on biodiversity and the environment, while encouraging structural financial reforms that instill morality, stability, and sustainability. We need to create a new definition of wealth beyond GDP, as well as an alternative model for money supply that demands less interest debt, that does not require unsustainable growth, and that does not encourage ordinary people or governments to live beyond their means. While we need to do this in a way and on a timeline that creates the least amount of disruption, we must approach such reforms with a mind to providing for a population yearning for greater meaning and a healthier social and spiritual environment.

In undertaking our examination to make changes for the better of humankind, we also need to understand the value of differing cultural perspectives, have a holistic and humble attitude, and embrace a view of society structured in such a way that we have the opportunity to rest and reflect, as well as work, balancing the worth of science and technology with the value of social and spiritual needs. Moreover, to create more harmony, in the spirit of tolerance and acceptance, we need to focus on common ground while putting economics, money, power, consumption, and material possessions in their appropriate places.

Further, we also need to comprehend that logic and rationality can only take us so far and how myth, ritual, and ceremony can help us reconnect to our spiritual dimension and guide our lives and society along a more fulfilling path.

We also need to understand our connection to nature and other species, and how these relate to our powerful mystical and social dimensions. Socially, we are hardwired to belong to tribes and communities and need to comprehend how to re-create the most essential connections in our everyday lives. We should also never forget that, as social animals connected to nature, happiness is derived primarily from having the close social relations of a family, friends, and community; feeling loved, useful, and valued by them; and having a meaningful life's purpose. We also need to understand the power and place of myth, ritual, and ceremony and how these can help to reconnect to a deeper spiritual life and guide the adaptation of our lives and society along a more fulfilling course.

We should listen to our hearts and the wisdom of nature, seeking to see as the Oglala Sioux holy man Black Elk when he had a vision, saying:

> . . . seeing in a sacred manner the shapes of all things in spirit, and *the shape of all shapes as they must live together like one being. And I saw the sacred hoop*[3] *of my people was one of many hoops that made one circle, wide as daylight and as starlight, and in the center grew one mighty flowering tree*[4] *to shelter all the children of one mother and one father. And I say it was holy.*[5] [Emphasis added]

Without a wiser basis for an appropriate course forward, there is justifiable fear that we may be approaching the tipping point in our impact on the environment and biodiversity on our little blue planet. We need to awaken to our obvious self-interest and take corrective action. To paraphrase Ishi, while we may be "clever," we must also be "wise" and use common sense in moving forward. Though we should face the challenges of the future with our intellects, we must also be guided by our hearts and the accumulated wisdom and knowledge of our ancestors.

In light of our current circumstances, if we wish to dance with our spirits, we must have a plan of constructive action that nurtures the human intuitive need to feel that we truly belong somewhere and are loved, and one that nourishes our spirits in a way that sustains hope. It would be a sad comment if a society of a supposed Stone Age man—Ishi—was able to build a more balanced and socially and spiritually more fulfilling life than exists in present-day society. I would like to end this book, as it started, with a prayer, in this case, one that I imagined may have been in Ishi's heart over 100 years ago.

ISHI'S PRAYER

Creator,
I beseech
as a humble servant
in the vast ocean of oblivion.

Thank you, Great Mystery,
for the gift of life
the blessing of awareness
and the caresses of your sweet grace.

Thank you, Infinite Wisdom,
for Mother Earth
the animals that feed and clothe
and the air, water, and plants that sustain.

Thank you, Great Spirit,
for the bonds of kin and community
the rituals, and myths that define
the small acts of kindness
and the fragrant love that nourishes our spirits.

Thank you, Sacred Being,
for each sweet breath of life
and the wonder of your universal presence.

Yet, Mighty Power,
I weep for the
sightless who act above nature
where the love of things and power blinds to the heart
or the times without peace and harmony.

Provide, Great Obscurity,
the soft kiss of knowledge
and the blessing of your mystical offerings.

Let us gather together, Holy Spirit,
under the Tree of Life
where the Grandfathers' wisdom can seep into our souls,
affirming an abiding respect for all
acting with one mind, one action, and one heart.

Help in your infinite kindness, Creator,
to avoid wanton suffering
and the ruin of the family, and tribe
as has been as my pitiful legacy
for which my heart will forever cry
in the darkness of folly.

Let there be understanding, Wise One,
of the coming season of change
where rains will rejuvenate
and ancient wisdom will guide
so our hearts will overflow
and we can once again
dance with our spirits.

NOTES

Preface

1. Butler, Caroline, and Charles Menzies. "Out of the Woods: Tsimishian Women in the Workforce," *Anthropology of Work Review*, 21, no. 2. June 28, 2008. www.ecoknow.ca/articles/awr_01.pdf.

2. Photo, the residence of Chief Dudoward, courtesy of the Provincial Archives, Victoria, BC, circa 1885. The house's design was based on a photograph of a home in eastern Canada.

3. The salmonberry bird is the name indigenous Canadian northwest coastal people gave to the bird known in English as the Swainson's thrush. The salmonberry bird's name derives from its annual arrival in May at the time when salmonberries ripen in the local forests. Native names of birds sometimes distill the essence of their appearance or behavior. In the Cherokee language, for instance, the meadowlark is called "star" because of the way the bird's tail spreads out when it soars. The Cherokee name for nuthatch is "deaf," possibly because of the bird's disregard for the presence of humans. Native names of birds also reflect a long affiliation between people and place. As writer Nancy Lord observes, "Words have power. Languages connected to place help us respect local knowledge, to ask and answer the tough questions about how the human and the nonhuman can live together in a tolerant and dignified way." http://www.birdnote.org/birdnote-transcript.cfm?id=767.

4. Otherwise known as the American robin (*Turdus migratorius*).

5. Known officially as black-capped chickadees.

6. The Steller's jay (*Cyanacitta Stelleri*) became British Columbia's official bird on December 17, 1987.

Introduction

1. Kroeber, Theodora. *Ishi in Two Worlds* (Berkeley: University of California Press, 2002; originally published in 1961), 9. A more recent source suggests: "Ishi apparently wasn't the last Yahi, according to new evidence from a UC Berkeley research archaeologist." Ishi was of mixed blood and was not pure Yahi according to new physical anthropological evidence. Even if this is true, Ishi still appears to have been the final surviving member of the last Yahi community that lived a traditional lifestyle on the land. http://www.berkeley.edu/news/media/releases/96legacy/releases.96/14310.html.

2. Ibid., 229.

3. Ibid., 237.

4. http://www.worldprayers.org/archive/prayers/meditations/i_do_not_think_that.html.

5. Peck, Don. "Can the Middle Class Be Saved?" *The Atlantic*, September 2011, 62.

6. http://www.stwr.org/poverty-inequality/key-facts.html.

7. Heaven, Pamela. "Repeat of 1931 on Horizon: Economists," *The Vancouver Sun*, June 27, 2012, C6.

8. http://www.quoteworld.org/quotes/4101.

9. Wehrein, Peter, ed. "Astounding Increase In Antidepressant Use by Americans," *Harvard Health Publications* (October 20, 2011). http://www.health.harvard.edu/blog/astounding-increase-in-antidepressant-use-by-americans-201110203624.

10. Wilkinson, Richard, and Kate Pickett. *The Spirit Level: Why Equality Is Good for Everyone* (London: Penguin Books, 2010). Graphic taken from http://www.equalitytrust.org.uk/resources/slides.

11. Comments of Tasunka Witko, or Crazy Horse, as he sat smoking the sacred pipe with Sitting Bull for the last time, 4 days before he was assassinated by being bayoneted by a guard in a military post in Nebraska. http://www.operationmorningstar.org/American percent20Indian percent20History percent20Overview.htm.

Chapter 1

1. Until some of the results of Greenspan's guidance became known as a result of the Great Recession of 2008, his tenure as chairman of the Federal Reserve was marked by considerable success. He prevented the 1987 stock market crash from spiraling into something much worse, in the 1990s presided over a long economic and financial market boom, and in the early 2000s supported policies that resulted in very low interest rates.

2. "25 People to Blame for the Financial Crisis," *Time*. http://www.time.com/time/specials/packages/article/0,28804,1877351_1877350_1877331,00.html.

3. http://www.brainyquote.com/quotes/keywords/abyss.html.

4. "Asia-Pacific Poised to Dominate North America as World's Top Ad Market, According to 'Most Comprehensive' Edition of the eMarketer Global Media Intelligence Report," October 10, 2012. http://www.emarketer.com/newsroom/index.php/asiapacific-poised-dominate-north-america-worlds-top-ad-market-comprehensive-edition-emarketer-global-media-intelligence-report.

5. Cross, Gary S. *An All-Consuming Century: Why Commercialism Won in America* (New York: Columbia University Press, 2000), 2.

6. GDP, or Gross Domestic Product, has been defined as the monetary value of all the finished goods and services produced within a country's borders in a specific time period, usually calculated on an annual basis. It includes all private and public consumption, government outlays, investments, and exports less imports that occur within a defined territory. In layman's terms, GDP is the economic measure that is commonly used as an indicator of the economic health of a country and a gauge to a country's standard of living.

   $$GDP = C + G + I + NX$$

   "**C**" is equal to all private consumption, or consumer spending, in a nation's economy

"**G**" is the sum of government spending

"**I**" is the sum of all the country's businesses spending on capital

"**NX**" is the nation's total net exports, calculated as total exports minus total imports. (NX = exports – imports) See: http://www.investopedia.com/terms/g/gdp.asp#axzz1hmXeiRg1. Another source points out that GDP initially referred to consumption of domestic production, but most products consumed are manufactured overseas so a dollar of consumer spending does not translate into a dollar of domestic production. This source also points out that the "consumer spending expenditures" also include expensive healthcare expenditures. See: http://www.businessweek.com/the_thread/economicsunbound/archives/2009/08/the_retail-impo.html.

7. Amadeo, Kimberly. "What are the components of GDP?" http://useconomy.about.com/od/grossdomesticproduct/f/GDP_Components.htm. In 2011, $10.726 trillion produced went toward household purchases.

8. Baily, Martin N., and Susan Lund. "American Hangover," *The International Economy* (Summer 2009), 24. http://www.international-economy.com/TIE_Su09_BailyLund.pdf.

9. Ibid., 24–25.

10. Dobbs, Richard, Andrew Grant, and Jonathan Woetsel. "Unleashing the Chinese Consumer," McKinsey Global Institute, September 5, 2009. http://www.mckinsey.com/Insights/MGI/In_the_news/Unleashing_the_Chinese_consumer.

11. America was not always a society whose economy was so completely wedded to personal consumption. In the early twentieth century, thrift was strongly encouraged, and consumption and unnecessary waste were discouraged. Such views emerged from an earlier time when ordinary people typically owned one or two sets of clothing and a single pair of shoes. For example, one of my English friends recalls how his great-grandfather (circa 1820) left his only linen shirt to a family member by a special provision in his will—considered such an important bequest that it merited singular reference in the document. This is in drastic contrast to the current situation where, in 2007, American consumers purchased a new piece of clothing every 5.4 days (Juliet B. Schor, *Plenitude* (New York: The Penguin Press, 2010), 29).

The attitudes of early American manufacturers were practical and aimed at providing items that were useful, durable, and easily fixable. When Henry Ford created his Model T car, he not only "saw his car as a great social leveler, a democratic one-size-fits-all symbol of American classlessness" but he also built it to be durable and reliable (Giles Slade, *Made to Break: Technology and Obsolescence in America* (Cambridge, MA: Harvard University Press, 2006), 30–31).

Giles Slade, in *Made to Break: Technology and Obsolescence in America*, noted that most engineers in the nineteenth century built their products to last, citing the example of a 114-year-old hand-blown carbon filament lightbulb made by Shelby Electric Company that still illuminates the fire hall in Livermore, California, after being originally switched on in 1901 (Slade, 30).

As the economy changed in the late nineteenth century from being based on man-powered to being based on machine-powered industry, manufacturers became aware that their factories could now produce more goods than could be readily distributed and consumed (Slade, 9–10). To address the problem of overproduction, they focused their efforts on creating more demand (and sustaining it) and better distribution (Slade, 11). Slade says:

Deliberate obsolescence in all of its forms—technological, psychological, or planned—is a uniquely American invention. Not only did we invent disposable products, ranging from diapers to cameras to contact lenses, but we invented the very concept of disposability itself, as a necessary precursor to our rejection of tradition and promotion of progress and change. As American manufacturers learned how to exploit obsolescence, American consumers increasingly accepted it in every aspect of their lives (Slade, 3–4).

For consumers, the short-term promise of increased consumption was the immediate gratification of owning something new that might create status and was stylish or luxurious. What emerged was a materialistic culture that evolved away from notions of frugality. Eventually, proponents of the ethic of durability and thrift were characterized as miserly penny-pinchers.

Writer T. J. Jackson Lears summarized the drift of American culture into increased consumption as having begun within the educated strata around the turn of the twentieth century. A bourgeois ethos that promoted perpetual work, compulsive saving, civic responsibility, and a rigid morality of self-denial transformed to a new set of values sanctioning periodic leisure, compulsive spending, apolitical passivity, and an apparently permissive but subtly coercive morality of individual fulfillment (Slade, 3).

12. "Americans Were 'Living in a Fool's Paradise' That's Gone Forever, George Soros," http://finance.yahoo.com/tech-ticker/article/228536/Americans-Were-percent22Living-in-a-Fool percent27s-Paradise percent22-That percent27s-Gone-Forever-Soros-Says?ticker s=^DJI,^GSPC,SPY,DIA,QQQQ,TLT; http://thesurvivalpodcast.com/forum/index.php?topic=4702.0; http://indurhedgefund.blogspot.ca/2009/04/americans-were-living-in-fools-paradise.html.

13. Kennedy, Robert F. "Remarks at the University of Kansas," March 18, 1968. http://www.poli-sci.utah.edu/~dlevin/AmPolTho/RFK@Kansas.pdf.

14. Clugston, Chris, "Excessive Consumption—America's Real Addiction," October 20, 2007. http://www.culturechange.org/cms/index.php?option=com_content&task=view&id=128&Itemid=1.

Chapter 2

1. http://www.brainyquote.com/quotes/keywords/growth.html.

2. Rowbotham, Michael. *The Grip of Death: A Study of Modern Money, Debt Slavery and Destructive Economics* (Charlbury, UK: Jon Carpenter Publishing, 2009), 5.

3. Ibid., 35.

4. Galbraith, John Kenneth. *Money: Whence It Came, Where It Went* (Boston: Houghton Mifflin, 1975), 15. http://www.legalforgery.com/pages/detail.php?section=27&id=152.

5. Rowbotham, Michael. *The Grip of Death*, 11.

6. Ibid., 12–13.

7. Korten, David C. *The Post-Corporate World: Life after Capitalism* (San Francisco: Berrett-Koehler, 1999), 24.

8. Rowbotham, Michael. *The Grip of Death*, 25.

9. Ibid., 27.

10. Perry, Geraldine, and Ken Fousek. *The Two Faces of Money* (Shelbyville, KY: Wasteland Press, 2007). http://www.thetwofacesofmoney.com/files/money.pdf, slide 12.

11. Anielski, Mark. *The Economics of Happiness: Building Genuine Wealth* (Gabriola Island, BC: New Society Publishers, 2009), 189.

12. As cited by Michael Rowbotham, *The Grip of Death*, 34–35, who, in turn, cites Charles Beard, *The Rise of American Civilisation* (London, J. Cape, 1927). Or see sources which dispute the authenticity of the quotation: http://www.monticello.org/site/jefferson/private-banks-quotation and http://www.markturner.net/2008/10/02/jeffersons-bogus-bank-quote-in-the-wild.

13. In fact, over 170 countries manage their economies through a central bank system coordinated by the Bank of International Settlements in Basil, Switzerland, with the Federal Reserve Bank being the de facto leader. Geraldine Perry and Ken Fousek, *The Two Faces of Money*. http://www.thetwofacesofmoney.com/files/money.pdf, slide 20.

14. Anielski, Mark. *The Economics of Happiness: Building Genuine Wealth*, 192.

15. Perry, Geraldine, and Ken Fousek. *The Two Faces of Money*. http://www.thetwofacesofmoney.com/files/money.pdf, slide 23.

16. As cited by Mark Anielski, *The Economics of Happiness: Building Genuine Wealth* (Gabriola Island, BC: New Society Publishers, 2009), 184–92.

17. Heinberg, Richard. *The End of Growth: Adapting to Our New Economic Reality* (Gabriola Island, BC: New Society Publishers, 2011), 2–3. http://www.amazon.ca/End-Growth-Adapting-Economic-Reality/dp/0865716951#reader_0865716951.

18. Buchanan, Patrick. "The Trade Issue Is Back, Big-Time," March 4, 2008, from Web site Real Clear Politics. http://www.realclearpolitics.com/articles/2008/03/the_second_battle_of_nafta.html.

19. Helin, Calvin. *The Economic Dependency Trap: Breaking Free to Self-Reliance* (St. Louis: Ravencrest Publishing, 2011), 51.

20. Apparently, this was a slight improvement over the $526 billion record in 2006 (more than twice as large as America's $224 billion bill for OPEC's oil).

21. Buchanan, Patrick. "The Trade Issue Is Back, Big-Time."

22. Original source for retiree data and chart: 2007 Social Security Trustees Report. http://72.14.253.104/search?q=cache:giPshMUtZtAJ:budget.senate.gov/democratic/charts/2007/Hearings/packet_Health percent2520Care_Orszag_062107.pdf+long-term+budget+shortfall+david+walker+2007&hl=en&ct=clnk&cd=4, Also see: http://www.cnbc.com/id/34941334/Will_Baby_Boomers_Bankrupt_Social_Security and http://www.bbhq.com/bomrstat.htm.

23. Savage, Luiza Ch. "Rescue Operation: Can the Canada Pension Fund Save the American Social Security System?" *Maclean's* magazine, June 18, 2007, 28–29. http://www.macleans.ca/article.jsp?content=20070618_106225_106225.

24. United Nations, "World Population to 2300," Department of Economic and Social Affairs, Population Division, New York, 2004, 5, 12. http://www.un.org/esa/population/publications/longrange2/WorldPop2300final.pdf.

25. Gray, Louise. "World's Population May Double by 2100, UN Warns," *The Vancouver Sun,* October 27, 2011, B5.

26. As summarized by Court Pearman, "Can the World Support an American Lifestyle?" *Epoch Times,* February 17, 2007, 6. http://en.epochtimes.com/news/7-2-12/51604.html. This was also the theme of his book: Lester R. Brown, *Plan B 2.0: Rescuing a Planet under Stress and a Civilization in Trouble* (New York: W. W. Norton & Company, Inc., 2006).

27. Ibid.

28. Ibid.

29. Swartz, Spencer, and Shai Oster. "China Tops U.S. in Energy Use," *The Wall Street Journal,* July 18, 2010. http://online.wsj.com/article/NA_WSJ_PUB:SB10001424052748703720504575376712353150310.html.

30. "China's Under-Consumption Over Stated," Finfacts Ireland Web site, September 16, 2009. http://www.finfacts.ie/irishfinancenews/article_1017904.shtml.

31. The chart is reproduced from data sets contained at Future of US China Trade.Com and Roundtable.Newamerica.net (New America Foundation Web site). Sources: http://www.futureofuschinatrade.com/fact/us-china-trade-data-household-consumption-share-of-GDP and http://roundtable.newamerica.net/sites/newamerica.net/files/articles/Slide2.PNG. Original sources for data are World Bank and International Monetary Fund.

32. Source, Anita. "Private consumption share of GDP expected to jump in China by 2015: Economist," *Global Times,* March 23, 2011. http://en.trade2cn.com/dataservice/110323155005n73-1.html. For a further discussion on this point, see: Richard Dobbs, "Unleashing the Chinese Consumer," *Newsweek International,* September 5, 2009. http://www.mckinsey.com/Insights/MGI/In_the_news/Unleashing_the_Chinese_consumer, or Samuel Sheridan, "Putting China's low household consumption in perspective," World Economic Roundtable, March 15, 2011. http://roundtable.newamerica.net/blogposts/2011/putting_china_s_low_household_consumption_in_perspective-46600 or Kai Guo and Papa N'Diaye, "Determinants of China's Private Consumption: An International Perspective," IMF Working Paper, WP/10/93, April 2010.

https://docs.google.com/viewer?a=v&q=cache:zRAeEPA_NHkJ:www.relooney.info/
SI_FAO-Asia/China_300.pdf+consumption+percent+of+gdp&hl=en&gl=ca&pid=bl&s-
rcid=ADGEESgvlHHNn1TqjEN-UvmWb0GmChBCzDEmRslWRCwIxZ8Bu0hq7c
Lrvp-B5PKKNVabY5rH6VN4y-pQJZSFHlK3PtjS3oconeid8bpSDypzdBFqx5beQTyg
USGv267As33ob9W5n5Qn&sig=AHIEtbTcvBWaeBQ3_xyhUT_GB4XXNSUYEw or
"China's consumption challenge," *The European Business Review.* http://www.european-
businessreview.com/?p=1195.

33. http://roundtable.newamerica.net/sites/newamerica.net/files/articles/Slide4.PNG.Origi-
nal source of data is the International Monetary Fund.

Chapter 3

1. http://www.usdebtclock.org. Figures from February 7, 2013.

2. Rowbotham, Michael. *Grip of Death: A Study of Modern Money, Debt Slavery and Destruc-
tive Economics* (Charlbury, UK: Jon Carpenter Publishing, 2009).

3. Pandurangi, Ashvin. "Our Depraved Future of Debt Slavery (Part I)," February 23, 2012.
http://www.marketoracle.co.uk/Article33279.html.

4. Rowbotham, Michael. *Grip of Death: A Study of Modern Money, Debt Slavery and Destruc-
tive Economics*, 1.

5. Ibid., 63–64.

6. Ibid., 4–5.

7. Anielski, Mark. *The Economics of Happiness: Building Genuine Wealth* (Gabriola Island, BC:
New Society Publishers, 2009), 185.

8. http://www.canada.com/vancouversun/news/story.html?id=b262e8d9-800c-49ec-966f-
4d71577c9a9a, http://www.webmd.com/balance/stress-management/news/20121018/
stress-parents-obesity-kids, http://www.medicalnewstoday.com, http://psychcentral.
com/news/2010/09/05/chronic-social-stress-linked-to-obesity/17685.html, and http://
www.medscape.org/viewarticle/562721.

9. http://www.naturalwellnesscare.com/stress-statistics.html and http://drronbittle.com/
custom_content/c_181600_1_stress_reliever_revealed.html. A further 54 percent of
Americans are concerned about the level of stress in their everyday work lives (American
Psychology Association Survey, 2004).

10. From 2010 survey of the American Psychological Association "Stress in America." http://
www.apa.org/news/press/releases/stress/key-findings.aspx.

11. Ibid.

12. http://www.cnn.com/2008/HEALTH/conditions/10/07/economic.stress/index.html.

13. From 2010 survey of the American Psychological Association "Stress in America." http://
www.apa.org/news/press/releases/stress/key-findings.aspx.

14. Ibid.

15. American Psychological Association, "Substance Abuse: The Nation's Number One Health Problem, But There Is Hope," June 2001, Vol. 32, No. 6. http://www.apa.org/monitor/jun01/subabuseone.aspx.

16. "Twenty Percent of Americans Risk Prescription Drug Addiction for Non-Medical Reasons," January 29, 2012. http://blog.drugrehabreferral.com/views/2012/01/29/twenty-percent-of-americans-risk-prescription-drug-addiction-for-non-medical-reasons.

17. Keith, David. "America's Fatal Addiction to Prescription Drugs," *The Guardian*, June 20, 2011. http://www.guardian.co.uk/commentisfree/cifamerica/2011/jun/10/prescription-drug-abuse.

18. Ibid. There are estimates of possible savings of at least $10 billion a year to be realized by Medicaid prescription drug benefit programs if such abuse was not occurring.

19. Fellner, Jamie. "Millions of Americans in Denial about Their Own Drug Abuse," http://www.drug-addiction.com/drugs_and_denial.htm.

20. http://wiki.answers.com/Q/Who_said_A_society_is_measured_by_how_it_treats_its_weakest_members.

21. Hope Yen. Associated Press, "Revised Government Formula Shows New Poverty High: 49.1M," November 7, 2011. Original source is updated U.S. census data. http://news.yahoo.com/revised-govt-formula-shows-poverty-high-49-1m-135427317.html or http://examiner-enterprise.com/sections/news/world/revised-government-formula-shows-new-poverty-high-491m.html.

22. Hope Yen. Associated Press. Article on 2010 census data titled "Census Finds Record Gap Between Rich and Poor," September 28, 2010. http://www.salon.com/2010/09/28/us_census_recession_s_impact_1. All data in this paragraph is from this source.

23. From 2010 analysis of Internal Revenue Service tax data by economist Emmanuel Saez of the University of California, Berkeley, as cited in David J. Lynch, "Growing income gap may leave U.S. vulnerable," October 13, 2011. http://www.bloomberg.com/news/2011-10-13/growing-income-divide-may-increase-u-s-vulnerability-to-financial-crises.html.

24. According to Arloc Sherman and Chad Stone, "Income gaps between very rich and everyone else more than tripled in last three decades," June 25, 2010, Centre on Budget and Policy Priorities, ". . . the gaps in after-tax income between the richest 1 percent of Americans and the middle and poorest fifths of the country more than tripled between 1979 and 2007." http://www.cbpp.org/cms/?fa=view&id=3220.

25. Kage, Ben. "United States Imprisons More People Than China, Russia or Any Other Nation, Experts Say," NaturalNews.com, December 13, 2006. http://www.naturalnews.com/021290.html.

26. Such astoundingly high incarceration rates have made America a "rogue state," according to Vivien Stern, research fellow at the prison studies center in London. Adam Liptak, "U.S. Prison Population Dwarfs That of Other Nations," the *New York Times*, April 23, 2008. http://www.nytimes.com/2008/04/23/world/americas/23iht-23prison.12253738.html?pagewanted=all.

27. Fellner, James. "US Addiction to Incarceration Puts 2.3 Million in Prison," December 1, 2006. http://hrw.org/english/docs/2006/12/01/usdom14728.htm. This number has risen from 411 to 491 sentenced inmates per 100,000 in the past 10 years.

28. Vicini, James. "More Americans Behind Bars Than Ever," *The Vancouver Sun*, February 29, 2008, A9. http://www.canada.com/story.html?id=c7380cc2-12a7-4327-955c-8b224164c50d.

29. Interview with Mark Shapiro, September 5, 2000. Online source. http://www.simulconference.com/clients/sowf/interviews/interview3.html or http://en.wikiquote.org/wiki/George_Soros.

30. Sandel, Michael J. "What Isn't for Sale?" *Atlantic* magazine, April 2012. Online source: http://www.theatlantic.com/magazine/archive/2012/04/what-isnt-for-sale/308902. All references to Michael Sandel in this subsection are from this article.

31. Ibid.

32. Ibid.

Chapter 4

1. Munro, Margaret. "Humanity 'Must Do More with Less'," *The Vancouver Sun*, May 13, 2011, B2. http://www2.canada.com/vancouversun/news/archives/story.html?id=11c3dfca-c0b5-4e16-b285-b6748bd16a39.

2. Phillips, Jack. "World Needs Vegetarian Diet by 2050, Says Report," *Epoch Times*, August–September 5, 2012, 1. The study was conducted by the Stockholm International Water Institute.

3. "Living standards to fall, OECD warns," *Vancouver Sun*, March 16, 2012. Another source suggests that the battle for resources will make the planet "unrecognizable" if the current trends continue. "Battle for Resources Will Make Earth 'Unrecognizable'," *The Vancouver Sun*, February 21, 2011, B3.

4. Munro, Margaret. "Humanity 'Must Do More with Less'."

5. Spencer, Richard. "China's Pollution Death Toll Revealed: 750,00 a Year," *The Vancouver Sun*, A1. The report titled "The Cost of Pollution in China" was conducted by international and Chinese government scientists. http://web.worldbank.org/WBSITE/EXTERNAL/COUNTRIES/EASTASIAPACIFICEXT/EXTEAPREGTOPENVIRONMENT/0,,contentMDK:21252897~pagePK:34004173~piPK:34003707~theSitePK:502886,00.html.

6. Valiant, John. *The Golden Spruce: A Story of Madness and Greed* (Toronto, Ontario: Vintage Canada, 2005), 81.

7. http://www1.american.edu/ted/ice/buffalo.htm.

8. Buffalo Field Campaign Web site. http://www.buffalofieldcampaign.org/aboutbuffalo/bisonnativeamericans.html. Apparently they ranged from the eastern seaboard to Oregon and California, and from Great Slave Lake in northern Alberta to northern Mexico.

9. http://www1.american.edu/ted/ice/buffalo.htm.

10. A global group whose members include nations, government agencies, nongovernmental organizations (NGOs), and thousands of scientists. http://www.iucn.org.

11. "More Than 16,300 Creatures Listed as At Risk of Extinction," *The Vancouver Sun*, September 13, 2007, A13.

12. Doyle, Alister. "Earth Losing 3 Species a Day, UN Says," *The Vancouver Sun*, May 23, 2007, A4.

13. Corwin, Jeff. "The Sixth Extinction," *Los Angeles Times*. November 30, 2009. http://articles.latimes.com/2009/nov/30/opinion/la-oe-corwin30-2009nov30.

14. Sample, Ian. "Yangtze River Dolphin Driven to Extinction," *Guardian Unlimited*, August 16, 2007. http://www.guardian.co.uk/environment/2007/aug/08/endangered species.conservation.

15. Ibid.

16. http://www.spiritbearyouth.org.

17. For further information, see: http://www.spiritbearyouth.org.

18. Zalasiewicz, Jan, Mark Williams, Alan Smith, et al. "Are We Now Living in the Anthropocene?" *GSA Today*, 18, No. 2 (February 2008). http://www.gsajournals.org/ perlserv/?request=get-toc&issn=1052-5173&volume=18&issue=2.

19. A fact that, in keeping with scholarly tradition, should result in the International Commission on Stratigraphy and its parent agency, the International Union of Geological Sciences, declaring this new boundary.

20. Boswell, Randy. "Humans Have Pushed the Planet into a New Geological Era, Experts Say," *The Vancouver Sun*, January 23, 2008, A5.

21. Marsden, William. "Humans Usher in Risky Age of Man," *The Vancouver Sun*, January 30, 2012, B5.

22. Based on the UN's World Meteorological Organization. Michael D. Lemonick, "CO_2 Hit Record High in 2011—UN Report," *The Guardian*, November 20, 2012. Online source: http://www.guardian.co.uk/environment/2012/nov/20/co2-record-high-2011-un-report. The International Energy Agency, an energy analysis group monitoring the world's most industrialized states, also reported that in 2011 CO_2 emissions hit all-time highs, further reducing the chances that the world might avoid a dangerous rise in global average temperatures by 2020. "Carbon Dioxide Emission Hit All-time High, Agency Reports," *The Vancouver Sun*, May 26, 2012, B11. As well, the International Energy Agency cautioned that the world was headed for a climate change crisis that can only be solved by exceptionally tough, immediate, and unprecedented international restraints in the consumption of fossil fuels. Scott Simpson, "Tough Fossil Fuel Curbs Urged," *The Vancouver Sun*, November 7, 2007, A1.

23. "Greenhouse Gas Beats Ancient Threshold," *The Vancouver Sun*, May 11, 2013, B4.

24. Zabarenko, Deborah. "Heat Could Kill 150,000 in U.S. Cities This Century," *Vancouver Sun*, May 25, 2012, B5. http://www2.canada.com/vancouversun/news/archives/story.

html?id=b73a171a-39fb-4685-ab40-d378644332e9. In the same vein, UN climate research-ers also warned that the planet could be perilously warm by more than previously expected, to 3.5 C, dangerously increasing the risk of both drought and flood. "Earth Could Warm by More Than 3.5 C, Leading to Extreme Weather: Research," *The Vancouver Sun*, May 25, 2012, B5.

25. Clavel, Guy. "Arctic Sees Major Ice-cap Retreat in 2 Years," *The Vancouver Sun*, January 24, 2008, A8. The original source is a report from the Paris-based National Centre for Scientific Research.

26. "The Melting North," special report, *The Economist*, June 16, 2012, 3. http://www.economist.com/node/21556798. In July 2012, NASA called the sharp rise in the melting of Greenland's ice sheet from 40 to 97 percent over a 4-day period "unprecedented" and "cause for grave concern." Seth Borenstein, "Greenland's Huge Ice Sheet Started Melting for a Short Period This Month," *The Vancouver Sun*, July 25, 2012, B4. A recent UN Inter-governmental Panel on Climate Change report advised that the world is veering toward a multicentury disaster "involving flood, famine, fire, drought, and disease" that can only be averted with a concerted global effort to curb CO_2 emissions. Scott Simpson, "Global Effort Needed to Avoid Environmental Disaster," *The Vancouver Sun*, November 17, 2007, A1.

27. "2012 Among Hottest: UN," *The Vancouver Sun*, November 29, 2012, B6. Source was the World Meteorological Organization.

28. "Oceans Getting Acidic at Unprecedented Rate," *The Vancouver Sun*, March 2, 2012, B5.

29. Welch, Craig. "CO_2 Eating Away at Marine Life Faster Than Expected: Scientists," *The Vancouver Sun*, March 7, 2012, B4. Washington Governor Chris Gregoire, concerned about the impact of acidification on the state's shellfish industry, signed an executive order directing state officials to work on the problem of ocean acidification. "Washington State Presses for Action on Ocean Acidity," *The Vancouver Sun*, November 29, 2012, B1.

30. Some of the impacts of falling pH levels are that sea urchin larvae change shape, squid me-tabolisms slow, some starfish and barnacles die, and the shells of oyster larvae dissolve while they are forming. Source: Ibid. A recent English study in the journal *Global Change Biology* found that ocean acidification caused by climate change is a trend likely to be felt most in polar regions resulting in disruption of marine food chains due to thinning of the protective shells of clams, sea urchins, mussels, oysters, lobsters, and crab. Source: Jim Drury, "Oceans' Rising Acid Levels Threaten Sea Life," *The Vancouver Sun*, August 8, 2012, B3.

31. The first 450 million years ago, the second 350 million years ago, the third and the fourth 200–250 million years ago, and the fifth 65 million years ago, when a giant meteor crashed into the Atlantic Ocean.

32. http://www.well.com/~davidu/sixthextinction.html.

Chapter 5

1. http://www.econlib.org/library/Smith/smWN.html.

2. Smith, Adam. *An Inquiry into the Nature and Causes of the Wealth of Nations*, Book 1, Chapter 2, 1776. http://geolib.com/smith.adam/won1-02.html.

3. http://www.econlib.org/library/Smith/smMS.html.

4. Kielburger, Craig, and Marc Kielburger, *Me to We. Turning Self-Help on Its Head* (Mississauga: John Wiley & Sons, Canada, 2004), 72.

5. Butler, Eamon. "The Morality of Capitalism," October 23, 2011. Online source: http://www.adamsmith.org/blog/tax-and-economy/the-morality-of-capitalism.

6. Miedma, Doug, and Lauren Tara Lacpra. "Outgoing Exec Rips Goldman Sachs," *The Vancouver Sun*, March 15, 2012. http://www.vancouversun.com/sports/Outgoing+exec+rips+Goldman+Sachs/6305703/story.html.

7. "Libor Stands for London Interbank Offered Rate. Bank CEO Faces Pressure to Resign as Inquiry Launched," *The Vancouver Sun*, July 3, 2012, B5; Howard Mustoe and Svenja O'Donnell, "Top Barclays Execs Resign Amid Scandal," *The Vancouver Sun*, July 4, 2012, C2.

8. "Despite High Profits HSBC Puts Aside Billions for Money Laundering Fines," *RT*, July 30, 2012. http://rt.com/business/news/hsbc-money-laundering-billion-375.

9. Fortado, Lindsay, Gavin Finch, and Liam Vaughan. "UBS's Rigging Fines Soar," *The Province*, December 20, 2012, A32.

10. Eaglesham, Jean, and Evan Perez. "UBS Let Off Too Easy, Critics Say," *The Wall Street Journal*, December 21, 2012, B8. http://online.wsj.com/article/SB10001424127887324731304578191801981480008.html.

11. Greil, Anita, and Marta Falconi. "Former UBS Official, Now Regulator, in Spotlight," *The Wall Street Journal*, December 20, 2012, A14.

12. "Standard Chartered Settles Iran Money Laundering Charges," August 14, 2011. http://www.usatoday.com/money/industries/banking/story/2012-08-14/standard-chartered-iran-money-laundering-settlement/57052122/1.

13. Ahmed, Kamal, and Jonathan Wynne-Jones. "Suicide of Deloitte Partner Daniel Pirron Linked to Standard Chartered's Iran Scandal," *The Telegraph*, August 22, 2012. http://www.telegraph.co.uk/finance/newsbysector/banksandfinance/9484442/Suicide-of-Deloitte-partner-Daniel-Pirron-linked-to-Standard-Chartereds-Iran-scandal.html.

14. "RBS Probed by U.S. Over Alleged Iran Sanction Violations—Report," *Mail* Online, August 22, 2012. http://www.dailymail.co.uk/news/article-2191878/RBS-probed-U-S-alleged-Iran-Sanction-violations-says-report.html.

15. Rappaport, Liz. "Banks Settles Iran Money Case," *The Wall Street Journal*, August 15, 2012. http://online.wsj.com/article/SB10000872396390444318104577589380427559426.html.

16. Manthorpe, Jonathan. "HSBC Struggles with Serving Higher Power and Earthly Demands," *The Vancouver Sun*, August 7, 2012, B8.

17. "Despite High Profits HSBC Puts Aside Billions for Money Laundering Fines," *RT*, July 30, 2012. http://rt.com/business/news/hsbc-money-laundering-billion-375. Pan Pylas and Pete Yost, "HSBC to Pay $1.9-billion Fine," *The Vancouver Sun*, December 12, 2012, C4.

18. Beucke, Dan. "Timely retirements, outrageous bonuses, and other epic executive handouts," *Bloomberg Businessweek*, December 21, 2011. http://www.businessweek.com/ finance/occupy-wall-street/archives/2011/12/timely_retirements_outrageous_bonuses_ and_other_epic_corporate_handouts.html.

19. Guest editorial from *Daily Telegraph*, "The Entire Global Trading System at Risk of Collapse," *The Vancouver Sun*, October 13, 2011, A16.

20. Editorial, "Lessons from the London Whale," *New York Times Sunday Review*, January 20, 2013, 10. http://www.nytimes.com/2013/01/20/opinion/sunday/lessons-from-the-london-whale.html?_r=0. A further recent article argued that banks need to have a straightforward standard of disclosure in commonsense terms that ordinary people can understand so that risky trading activities can be evaluated and that there be a real risk of punishment for bank executives who mislead investors. Frank Partnoy and Jesse Etinger, "What's inside America's banks?" *The Atlantic*, January/February 2013, 70.

Chapter 6

1. http://www.brainyquote.com/quotes/quotes/g/geoffreych165940.html.

2. As cited by Clifford A. Pickover, *Time: A Traveler's Guide* (New York: Oxford University Press, 1998), ix. http://bit.ly/A3IoMp. (Original source was OMNI, 1994.)

3. Angelus Silesius, translated, introduced, and drawn by Fredrick Franck, *Messenger of the Heart: The Book of Angelus Silesius* (Bloomington, Indiana: World Wisdom Inc., 2005), 39. http://books.google.ca/books?id=zmBPI4aakLAC&pg=PA39&dq=Time+is+of+your+ own+making+silesius&hl=en&sa=X&ei=y2YYUbSLFMbOiwKzhYG4DA&ved=0C C4Q6AEwAA#v=onepage&q=Time%20is%20of%20your%20own%20making%20 silesius&f=false or http://www.notable-quotes.com/t/time_quotes.html.

4. http://en.wikipedia.org/wiki/Time.

5. Wells, Cheryl. "Suns, Moons, Clocks, and Bells: Native Americans and Time," University of Wyoming, Department of History, December 1, 2008, 1. http://www-bcf.usc. edu/~philipje/USC_History_Seminar/Wells/Wells_SUNS_MOONS_reading.pdf.

6. Ibid., 4. A lot of what matters to people in the current society didn't matter to Native Americans.

7. "Perception of Time Pressure Impairs Performance," *Science Daily*, February 16, 2009. http://www.sciencedaily.com/releases/2009/02/090210162035.htm.

8. Dedyna, Kathryn. "Workaholic 'Less Content with Life'," *The Vancouver Sun*, August 11, 2007, A4. http://www2.canada.com/saskatoonstarphoenix/news/business/story.html?id= 7dd67354-73ca-4133-a73d-69cce3f0543c&p=1. The data comes from a study of workers ages 19 to 64 based on a 2005 general social survey by Statistics Canada.

9. Ibid. According the Workaholics Anonymous Web site, some of the signposts of workaholism are difficulty in loving or accepting ourselves and using work as a way of gaining approval; not acknowledging feelings; using work as a way to deal with the uncertainties and stress of life. http://www.workaholics-anonymous.org/page.php?page=signposts.

10. Gallup, Inc., asked 1,000 people in each of 150 countries about their happiness and found that seven of the world's 10 countries with the most upbeat attitudes were in Latin America. The Associated Press, "Rich Countries Are Not the Happiest," *The Province*, December 20, 2012, A38.

11. Louv, Richard. *Last Child in the Woods* (Algonquin Books of Chapel Hill: New York, 2005), 175.

Chapter 7

1. Black Elk. Originally from *The Sacred Pipe*. http://www.rodneyohebsion.com/native-american-proverbs-quotes.htm#religions.

2. He arrived in America in 1897.

3. http://www.goodreads.com/quotes/tag/oneness.

4. http://www.thefreedictionary.com/atomistic.

5. http://www.merriam-webster.com/dictionary/atomistic.

6. Lecture by Rudolf Steiner, "Man's Position in the Cosmic Whole, the Platonic World-Year," Dornach, January 28, 1917, GA 174, published in *Anthroposophic News Sheet*, Nos. 1–2 (January 1940). http://wn.rsarchive.org/Lectures/ManPos_index.html.

7. Ibid.

8. Jung Young Lee. *The Principle of Changes: Understanding the I Ching* (New York: University Books, 1971), 53–54.

9. Ibid., 55–56.

10. Briggs, John, Ph.D., and F. David Peat, Ph.D. *Seven Lessons of Chaos: Timely Wisdom for the Science of Change* (New York: Harper Collins, 1999), 152. They suggest further that this separation took place based on a modern mechanistic paradigm which has led to the modern wasteland of so-called progress and unlimited growth.

Chapter 8

1. http://www.brainyquote.com/quotes/quotes/a/abrahamlin103270.html.

2. Known as the Aristotelian scientific view.

3. In 1530, Copernicus completed and gave to the world his great work *De Revolutionibus*, which asserted that the earth rotated on its axis once daily and traveled around the sun once yearly: a fantastic concept for the time. Up to the time of Copernicus, thinkers of the Western world believed in the Ptolemaic theory that the universe was a closed space bounded by a spherical envelope beyond which there was nothing. Claudius Ptolemy, an Egyptian living in Alexandria at about AD 150, organized the thoughts of the earlier thinkers. One of the ancient Greek astronomers, Aristarchus, did have ideas similar to those more fully developed by Copernicus, but they were rejected in favor of the geocentric, or earth-centered, scheme espoused by Aristotle. Ptolemy's findings were that the earth was a fixed, inert, immovable mass located at the center of the universe, and all celestial bodies,

including the sun and the stars, revolved around it. This theory appealed to human nature, fitting with casual observations people make in the field and feeding their egos. http://www.blupete.com/Literature/Biographies/Science/Copernicus.htm.

4. http://thinkexist.com/quotations/arrogance/2.html.

5. That is, an American billion with nine zeros as opposed to a UK billion with 12 zeros.

6. Brit, Robert Roy. "Universe Measured: We're 156 Billion Light-years Wide!" CNN.com, May 24, 2004. http://www.cnn.com/2004/TECH/space/05/24/universe.wide/index.html.

7. Multiply 156 billion by 5.88 trillion miles, the distance that light travels in a vacuum in 1 year.

8. http://www.theorderoftime.com/science/galactic.html.

9. http://www.kidcyber.com.au/topics/dino_eras.htm. Beginning 245 million years ago in the Triassic period and becoming extinct toward the end of the Cretaceous period.

10. http://people.hsc.edu/faculty-staff/maryp/Core/homo_erectus_to_homo_sapiens.htm.

11. Jung Young Lee. *The Principle of Changes: Understanding the I Ching* (New York: University Books, 1971), 9.

12. Ibid.

Chapter 9

1. "Time: A Traveller's Guide," 12. http://bit.ly/AtPIXV.

2. As cited by Krista Tippet in *Einstein's God: Conversation about Science and the Human Spirit* (New York: Penguin Group, 2006), 124–25.

3. Jung Young Lee. *The Principle of Changes: Understanding the I Ching* (New York: University Books, 1971), 2–3.

4. http://thinkexist.com/quotations/technology.

5. http://rescomp.stanford.edu/~cheshire/EinsteinQuotes.html.

6. Speech of 1959. John F. Kennedy lived from 1917–1963 and was the thirty-fifth president of the United States from 1961 to 1963. http://www.searchquotes.com/quotation/I_am_sorry_to_say_that_there_is_too_much_point_to_the_wisecrack_that_life_is_extinct_on_other_planet/3010.

Chapter 10

1. McLuhan, Marshall. *Understanding Media: The Extensions of Man*, 2nd ed. (New York: McGraw-Hill Book Company, 1964), 23.

2. "Students Lose Sense of Self When Unplugged," *The Vancouver Sun*, April 2, 2011, B1. http://www2.canada.com/vancouversun/news/archives/story.html?id=408221a1-8eef-4503-b318-1f8c973b0570. The study was conducted by the International Center for Media and the Public Agenda at the University of Maryland. The results were consistent,

no matter what regions of the world the students came from or what disparities in economic development, culture, and political governance existed.

3. Harris, Misty. "Canadians Dependent on Smartphones; Survey," *The Vancouver Sun*, December 27, 2012, B1.

4. Cooper, Glenda. "Convenient Technology Transforms Social Mores," *The Vancouver Sun*, December 8, 2012, E3.

5. Ibid.

6. Erler, Alexandre. "Should we be afraid of virtual reality?" Practical Ethics, University of Oxford. http://www.practicalethicsnews.com/practicalethics/2009/09/should-we-be-afraid-of-virtual-reality.html.

7. Ibid.

8. Brown, Eryn. "Brain Changes Linked to Video Games," *The Vancouver Sun*, November 16, 2011, B3.

9. Highfield, Roger. "Virtual Worlds 'Could Replace Real Relationships'," *The Telegraph*, June 19, 2007. http://www.telegraph.co.uk/news/uknews/1554999/Virtual-worlds-could-replace-real-relationships.html and http://technology.timesonline.co.uk/tol/news/tech_and_web/the_web/article5139532.ece.

10. Ibid.

11. Erler, Alexandre. "Should we be afraid of virtual reality?" http://www.practicalethicsnews.com/practicalethics/2009/09/should-we-be-afraid-of-virtual-reality.html.

12. http://www.csun.edu/science/health/docs/tv&health.html. Representing a value for that time, assuming an average wage of $5/hour, of $1.25 trillion dollars. Comparatively, the average child watches television for 28 hours per week, while the average American youth spends 1,500 hours per year watching television (versus 900 hours in school). Millions of Americans are so hooked on television that their behavior fits the criteria for substance abuse as defined in the official psychiatric manual, according to Rutgers University psychologist and TV-Free America board member Robert Kubey. Heavy TV viewers exhibit six dependency symptoms—two more than necessary to arrive at a clinical diagnosis of substance abuse. These include: 1) using TV as a sedative; 2) indiscriminate viewing; 3) feeling loss of control while viewing; 4) feeling angry with oneself for watching too much; 5) inability to stop watching; and 6) feeling miserable when kept from watching. According to another study from the University of California, Berkeley, researchers found that Americans also spend nine times more time watching television and movies than they spend on physical activities and exercise, contributing, no doubt, to increasing obesity and diabetes. Alisa Tanphanich, "U.S. TV Time Far Exceeds Time Spent on Exercise," *The Daily Californian,* Wednesday, March 31, 2004. http://archive.dailycal.org/printable.php?id=14717.

13. Blodget, Henry. "IBM Survey: Time Spent on Internet Now Rivals TV," August 22, 2007. http://www.alleyinsider.com/2007/08/ibm-survey-time.html. See also: Mike Sachoff,

"Internet Outpacing TV for Time Spent: TV Viewing Losing Ground," posted February 19, 2008. http://www.webpronews.com/topnews/2008/02/19/internet-outpacing-tv-for-time-spent. Specifically, 19 percent said they spend 6-plus hours a day online (versus only 9 percent who watch 6-plus hours of TV), and 60 percent said they spend 1 to 4 hours a day online (versus 66 percent who watch 1 to 4 hours of TV).

14. http://www.csun.edu/science/health/docs/tv&health.html. This Web site, in turn, cites "Compiled by TV-Free America," 1322 18th Street, NW, Washington, D.C. 20036. Unless otherwise indicated, all references to television in this section are from this source. As well, 99 percent of households possess at least one television, and there are 2.24 TV sets in the average U.S. household with over 66 percent of U.S. homes with three or more TV sets.

15. Louv, Richard. *Last Child in the Woods: Saving Our Children from Nature-Deficit Disorder* (New York: Algonquin Books of Chappell Hill, 2006), 34.

16. Ibid., 65–66.

17. Ibid.

18. http://quotes.dictionary.com/it_is_a_medium_of_entertainment_which_permits.

Chapter 11

1. http://myweb.cwpost.liu.edu/paievoli/finals/505Sp_03/Prj1/irene_piechota.htm.

2. J. B. Sykes, ed. *The Concise Oxford Dictionary*, 7th ed. (New York: Oxford University Press, 1984), 189.

3. Private correspondence, April 14, 2008. His business Web site can be located at http://www.praxistech.com.

4. Fralic, Shelley. "Can't Change a Tire or Sew on a Button? When Did We Become So Helpless?" *The Vancouver Sun*, May 2, 2012, A6. Nearly half of the women surveyed said they couldn't change a tire.

5. http://au.answers.yahoo.com/answers2/frontend.php/question?qid=20080306101717A AXyESH.

6. As recounted by David G. Myers, *Psychology* (New York: Worth Publishers, 2003), 338–39.

7. Huessmann, L. Rowell, Jessica Mosie-Titus, Cheryl-Lynn Podolski, and Leonard D. Eron, University of Michigan, "Longitudinal relations between children's exposure to TV violence and their aggressive and violent behavior in young adulthood: 1977–1992," *Developmental Psychology*, 2003, Vol. 39, No. 2, 201–21. http://academic.udayton.edu/RondaScant-lin/CMM449_Fall2003/Comm449_Fall/3_Topic3/Media_Violence_March2003.pdf, http://www.jacksonkatz.com/PDF/ChildrenMedia.pdf, http://www.aafp.org/online/en/home/policy/policies/v/violencemedia.html, and http://www.aacap.org/cs/root/develop-mentor/the_impact_of_media_violence_on_children_and_adolescents_opportunities_for_clinical_interventions.

8. Gentle, Douglas A., and Craig A. Anderson. *Media Violence and Children*, Chapter 7, "Violent Video Games: The Newest Media Violence Hazard" (Westport, Connecticut:

Praeger, 2003), 151. http://www.psychology.iastate.edu/faculty/caa/abstracts/2000-2004/03GA.pdf.

Chapter 12

1. Schopmeyer, Kim D., and Bradley J. Fisher. "Insiders and Outsiders: Exploring Ethnocentrism and Cultural Relativity in Sociology Courses," *Teaching Sociology*, Vol. 21, 1993 (April: 148–53), 148. http://www.jstor.org/pss/1318635.

2. http://thinkexist.com/quotes/with/keyword/american_language.

3. Jung Young Lee. *The Principle of Changes: Understanding the I Ching* (New York: University Books, 1971), 3. All information on the *I Ching* in this paragraph is from this source.

4. Ibid., 1.

5. Kroeber, Theodora. *Ishi in Two Worlds* (Berkeley: University of California Press, 2004), xi. http://books.google.ca/books?id=4eRL24p4uwkC&printsec=frontcover&source=gbs_ge_su mmary_r&cad=0#v=onepage&q&f=false.

6. Miner, Horace. "Body Ritual among the Nacirema," *The American Anthropologist*, Vol. 58, Issue 3, 1956, 503–07. http://onlinelibrary.wiley.com/doi/10.1525/aa.1956.58.3.02a00080/ abstract, https://www.msu.edu/~jdowell/miner.html?pagewanted=al.

7. Ibid., 503.

8. Ibid.

9. Ibid.

10. Ibid., 506.

11. Alan Dundes, ed. *Every Man His Way: Readings in Cultural Anthropology* (Englewood Cliffs, New Jersey: Prentice-Hall, 1968), 433, as cited by Lyn Thomas, "Student Reactions to Horace Miner's Body Ritual Among the Nacirema," 3. Online source: http:// www.anthropology.pomona.edu/html/Faculty/lthomas/Thomas_1994-BodyRitual.pdf. Also see: http://offoxesandhedgehogs.wordpress.com/2012/01/29/rituals-of-the-nacirema-must-read-article-before-summaries-underneath, http://1020isawesome.pbworks.com/w/page/ 4732848/Reading%20Response%2013, http://www.studymode.com/subjects/nacirema-page1. html, and http://duca94.wordpress.com/2011/05/22/reading-review-body-ritual-among-the-nacirema.

12. http://www.brainyquote.com/quotes/authors/c/charles_darwin.html.

13. http://quotationsbook.com/quote/9484.

14. Squires, Nick. "Drought Leads Australians to Seek Ancient Aboriginal Solutions," *The Vancouver Sun*, May 5, 2007, A12. Prolonged droughts have enormous impacts on regions of the nation, and knowing when it might rain is critical. A recent media report noted that:

> Where modern meteorologists base their forecasts on satellites and synoptic charts, aborigines observe the flight of black cockatoos and the flowering of wattle bushes. And they say a change in the weather is coming.

"The cockys [cockatoos] are flocking everywhere. That's usually a good sign that rain is coming," said Jeremy Clark, an Aborigine park ranger from the south of the country. "The way the flora and plants and shrubs are starting to react, I'd certainly be expecting rain."

The weather philosophy of Aborigines is based on the principle that subtle change to plants and animals provide clues to changes in the weather. Apparently residents of the southern and most populated parts of the country can now consult the Indigenous Weather Knowledge on the official Web site of Australia's Bureau of Meteorology. Also see: http://www.bom.gov.au/iwk.

15. National Geographic News: Reporting Your World Daily. http://news.nationalgeographic. com/news/2002/06/0627_020628_wadedavis.html.

16. Sanford, Katherine. "Losses for Words," *Up Here* magazine, 24, No. 3 (April–May, 2008), 51.

17. Ibid.

18. http://quotationsbook.com/quote/26811.

Chapter 13

1. http://www.trivia-library.com/a/36th-us-president-lyndon-b-johnson.htm.

Chapter 14

1. Twist, Lynne. *The Soul of Money: Transferring Your Relationship with Money and Life* (New York: W. W. Norton & Company, 2003). http://www.amazon.com/o/ASIN/0393050971/ ref=nosim/thesoulofmone-20#reader_0393050971, and http://www.soulofmoney.org/about/ about-the-book.

2. Ibid., 20–21. Also as summarized by Mark Anielski, *The Economics of Happiness* (Gabriola Island, BC: New Society Publishers, 2009), 179–80.

3. Ibid., 8.

4. Anileski, *The Economics of Happiness*, 189.

5. http://en.wikipedia.org/wiki/JAK_Members_Bank, http://www.feasta.org/documents/ review2/carrie2.htm, and http://www.youtube.com/watch?v=aW2pj109Cr8.

6. http://en.wikipedia.org/wiki/Local_exchange_trading_system, http://www.letslinkuk.net, and http://www.lets-linkup.com.

7. A market economy is one in which decisions regarding investment, production, and distribution are based on supply and demand—the prices of goods and services are determined in a free price system—whereas a planned economy is one where investment and production decisions are embodied in a planned matrix of production.

Chapter 15

1. As discussed by Mark Anielski, *The Economics of Happiness* (Gabriola Island, BC: New Society Publishers, 2009), 16.

2. Ibid.

3. Ibid., 54–55. Aristotle also thought that economics was concerned with the well-being of the household and should be the science of family and household stewardship.

4. http://chinese.yabla.com/chinese-english-pinyin-dictionary.php?define=Xiaokang, and http://en.wikipedia.org/wiki/Xiaokang.

5. http://www.thegoddards.ca/alexgoddardblog/?p=1066, http://www.royalroads.ca/rrunews/greening-china, and http://cmp.hku.hk/2007/09/19/622.

6. Anielski, Mark. *The Economics of Happiness*, 53.

7. Ibid., 54.

8. Ibid.

9. http://www.livinglifefully.com/nativeamericanwisdom.htm.

10. Ibid.

11. http://www.indigenouspeople.net/quotes.htm.

Chapter 16

1. The predecessor of GDP is Gross National Product (GNP). The notions of GDP and GNP are similar in that they represent the size and strength of an economy, but their definition, calculations, and applications are different. In effect, GDP and GNP are cousins and often used interchangeably by noneconomists.

2. The following are three approaches to determining GDP:

   Expenditure Method
   GDP = all expenditures incurred by individuals during 1 year.

   Production Approach
   GDP = market value of all final goods and services calculated during 1 year.

   Income Approach
   GDP = sum total of all the incomes of individuals living in a country during a year.

   Comparatively, GNP = GDP + NR (net income from assets abroad).

3. Anielski, Mark. *The Economics of Happiness*, 2.

4. Online source: http://www.pembina.org/pub/58.

5. This was developed by the San Francisco–based economic policy think tank Redefining Progress. http://rprogress.org/index.htm.

6. It seeks to reflect social and environmental depreciation costs, attempting to measure well-being according to what people define as progress.

7. Anielski, Mark. *The Economics of Happiness*, 5.

8. Ibid., 21, 65.

9. Ibid., 67, 74–77.

Chapter 17

1. Jackson, Tim, and Peter Victor. "Prosperity without Growth Is Possible," *The Vancouver Sun*, September 19, 2011, A11.

2. Ibid.

3. Leggett, Jeremy. "Prosperity without Growth: Economics for a Finite Planet by Tim Jackson," *The Guardian*, January 23, 2010. http://www.guardian.co.uk/books/2010/jan/23/prosperity-without-growth-tim-jackson. It is argued that we might be able to continue to decouple GNP growth from resource use if we become more efficient in the use of resources. However, Jackson suggests the problem with this reasoning is that if we continue to grow GNP, we continue to increase the emission of greenhouse gases, resulting in diminishing prosperity.

4. Pearlman, Jonathan. "Mining Magnate Is World's Richest Woman," *The Vancouver Sun*, May 26, 2012, B8. All statistics and information in this paragraph are cited from this source.

5. This was done for purposes of gathering inside information about politicians and celebrities to sensationalize reports in its British tabloid.

6. Andersen, Kurt. "The Protestor," *Time*, December 14, 2012. http://www.time.com/time/specials/packages/article/0,28804,2101745_2102132_2102373-2,00.html.

7. Perreaux, Les. "A Mystery: Why Jean Charest Chose to Blink the First Time Out," *The Globe and Mail*, June 2, 2012, F6.

8. Clarke, Ken. "Punish the Feral Rioters, But Address Our Social Deficit Too," *The Guardian*, September 5, 2011. http://www.guardian.co.uk/commentisfree/2011/sep/05/punishment-rioters-help.

9. Ibid. Ken Clarke, the Conservative MP for Rushcliffe and minister without portfolio, is a former lord chancellor and secretary of state for justice.

10. Schor, Juliet B. *Plenitude* (New York: The Penguin Press, 2010).

11. Ibid., 16.

Chapter 18

1. His Holiness the Dalai Lama. *Ancient Wisdom, Modern World* (London: Abacus, 2006), 4.

Chapter 19

1. Woods, Sarah. "Horses Have a Sixth Sense to Pick Up on Anxiety, Research Has Shown," *Horse & Hound*, July 17, 2009. http://www.horseandhound.co.uk/news/397/286372.html. Also see: http://animaluniversity.com/2010/do-horses-have-a-sixth-sense.

2. Mott, Maryann. "Did Animals Sense the Tsunami Was Coming?" *National Geographic News*, January 4, 2005. http://news.nationalgeographic.com/news/2005/01/0104_050104_tsunami_animals.html. Also, see: http://www.foxnews.com/story/0,2933,143737,00.html, http://blogs.discovery.com/animal_oddities/2011/03/can-animals-sense-earthquakes-and-

tsunamis.html, http://www.arkanimals.com/dlg/tsunami_earthquake_animal_pre-diction.htm, and http://science.howstuffworks.com/environmental/life/zoology/all-about-animals/pet-sixth-sense1.htm.

3. http://www.pbs.org/wnet/nature/episodes/killers-in-eden/introduction/1048

4. According to the *Merriam-Webster's Dictionary*, the baleen whale is a suborder of *Mysticeti*, a large whale lacking teeth but able to filter small crustaceans out of large quantities of seawater; suborder includes humpback, blue, fin, minke, and right whales. http://www.merriam-webster.com/dictionary/baleen percent20whale.

5. Such as those of the Nuu-cha-nulth tribe from the west coast of Vancouver Island, who are renowned for their whaling culture.

6. The information used in this discussion is from the ABC documentary *Killers in Eden* (produced by Klaus Toft) and from the Web sites listed. http://www.killersofeden.com.

7. Ibid.

Chapter 20

1. Berreby, David. *Us and Them: Understanding Your Tribal Mind* (New York: Little, Brown, and Company, 2005), 327.

2. Goleman, Daniel. *Social Intelligence: The New Science of Human Relationships* (New York: Bantam Dell, 2006).

3. Ibid. He suggests that "'The social brain is the sum of the neural mechanisms that orchestrate our interactions as well as our thoughts and feelings about people and our relationships" (10). He refers to scholarly articles, discussing a newly discovered class of neurons that guide snap social decisions; a different variety of brain cells that sense moods, emotions, and potential actions of other people and prepare us to empathize and imitate those people; and brain secretions of dopamine that cause pleasure if specific social cues occur (9).

4. Berreby, David. *Us and Them*, 43–44.

5. Ibid.

6. Ibid., 63.

7. Ibid., 331.

8. http://psychology.about.com/od/nindex/g/needtobelong.htm.

9. Berreby, David. *Us and Them*, 223.

10. http://www.efmoody.com/miscellaneous/loneliness.html.

11. Klinenberg, Eric. "Solo nation: American consumers stay single," CNNMoney, January 25, 2012. http://finance.fortune.cnn.com/2012/01/25/eric-klinenberg-going-solo. Also see Stephen Marche, "Is Facebook Making Us Lonely?" *The Atlantic*, May 2012, 60.

12. http://www.efmoody.com/miscellaneous/loneliness.html.

13. "Loneliness is getting rampant in America," Softpedia. http://news.softpedia.com/news/Loneliness-Is-Getting-Rampant-in-America-27518.shtml.

14. Marche, Stephen. "Is Facebook Making Us Lonely?" 64.

15. Cherry, Kendra. "Loneliness." http://psychology.about.com/od/psychotherapy/a/loneliness.htm. Larry Husten, "The grim impact of living alone," *Forbes*, June 18, 2012. http://www.forbes.com/sites/larryhusten/2012/06/18/the-grim-impact-of-loneliness-and-living-alone.

16. Marche, Stephen. "Is Facebook Making Us Lonely?" 64.

17. Ibid., 64. Original source is a paper by Ronald Dworkin prepared for the Hoover Institution.

18. Figure 25 was provided by Te Taru White, one of the foremost experts on Maori culture and traditions, former joint leader and curator of Te Papa, Aotearoa New Zealand's National Museum, and chief executive of Te Puia, New Zealand's National Maori Arts and Crafts Institute.

Chapter 21

1. http://www.afriprov.org/index.php/african-proverb-of-the-month/23-1998proverbs/137-november-1998-proverb.html, or http://en.wikipedia.org/wiki/It_Takes_a_Village.

2. Le Roux, Marriette. "Working Cooperatively Led to Bigger Brain Size, Study Suggests," *The Vancouver Sun*, April 11, 2012, B7.

3. Cited by Stephen Marche, "Is Facebook Making Us Lonely?" *The Atlantic*, May 2012, 67–68.

4. Ibid., 69.

Chapter 22

1. Online source: http://dictionary.reference.com/browse/myth.

2. All references to Joseph Campbell in the remainder of this chapter were transcribed from the PBS series *The Power of Myth*. http://video.pbs.org/video/2201676017.

3. Ibid.

4. Ibid.

5. As summarized by Greg Doherty in "Joseph Campbell's Four Functions of Mythology." http://drake.marin.k12.ca.us/staff/doherty/fourfunctionsmythology.html.

6. http://oxforddictionaries.com/definition/english/ritual.

7. http://www.quotecosmos.com/subjects/170/Ceremony.

8. http://www.brainyquote.com/quotes/keywords/ritual.html.

9. http://en.wikiquote.org/wiki/Xun_zi

10. Cited by John F. Bryde, Ph.D., *Modern Indian Psychology*, rev. ed. (Vermillion, SD: Institute of Indian Studies, The University of South Dakota, 1971), 86.

Conclusion

1. Jung Young Lee, in *The Principle of Changes: Understanding the I Ching* (New York: University Books, 1971), states: "Everything in the universe is regarded as the interaction of

heaven and earth. This idea is implicit in the word 'I' 易"(20). He goes on to suggest, "The word 'Ching' [经] when used in the classic signifies the wrapping of words . . . 'wei' [literally means 'woof' of a fabric] and 'ching' are used to denote . . . threads of knowledge, which, woven together, were regarded by the Chinese as a unified fabric covering all human knowledge" (41—42). Taken together, he suggests further, "The core of the I Ching is no doubt the principle of 'I' [whereas] . . . 'Ching' signifies merely a book or a classic of literature. Therefore, the 'I Ching' is nothing more than a book about . . . change . . . Thus the theoretical foundation of the 'I Ching' is based on this principle of changes" (53).

2. Ibid., 2–3.

3. The sacred hoop is based on the Sioux concept that everything in the universe is interrelated, that human beings and all things which exist in their environment are connected in one continuous process of growth and development.

4. The flowering tree is symbolic of growth and prosperity for all people.

5. Neihardt, John G. *Black Elk Speaks* (New York: Excelsior Editions, 2008), 33.

BIBLIOGRAPHY

Newspapers, Unpublished Materials, Articles, and Books

"2012 Among Hottest: UN," *The Vancouver Sun*, November 29, 2012.

Andersen, Kurt. "The Protestor," *Time*, December 14, 2012.

Anielski, Mark. *The Economics of Happiness: Building Genuine Wealth* (Gabriola Island, BC: New Society Publishers, 2009).

"Battle for Resources Will Make Earth 'Unrecognizable'," *The Vancouver Sun*, February 21, 2011.

Blodget, Henry. "IBM Survey: Time Spent on Internet Now Rivals TV," August 22, 2007.

Borenstein, Seth. "Greenland's Huge Ice Sheet Started Melting for a Short Period This Month," *The Vancouver Sun*, July 25, 2012.

Boswell, Randy. "Humans Have Pushed the Planet into a New Geological Era, Experts Say," *The Vancouver Sun*, January 23, 2008.

Briggs, John, Ph.D., and F. David Peat, Ph.D. *Seven Lessons of Chaos: Timely Wisdom for the Science of Change* (New York: Harper Collins, 1999).

Brown, Eryn. "Brain Changes Linked to Video Games," *The Vancouver Sun*, November 16, 2011.

Brown, Lester R. *Plan B 2.0: Rescuing a Planet under Stress and a Civilization in Trouble* (New York: W. W. Norton & Company, Inc., 2006).

Bryde, John F., Ph.D. *Modern Indian Psychology*, rev. ed. (Vermillion, SD: Institute of Indian Studies, The University of South Dakota, 1971).

Butler, Caroline, and Charles Menzies. "Out of the Woods: Tsimshian Women in the Workforce," *Anthropology of Work Review*, 21, no. 2. June 28, 2008.

"Carbon Dioxide Emission Hit All-time High, Agency Reports," *The Vancouver Sun*, May 26, 2012.

Clarke, Ken. "Punish the Feral Rioters, But Address Our Social Deficit Too," *The Guardian*, September 5, 2011.

Clavel, Guy. "Arctic Sees Major Ice-Cap Retreat in 2 Years," *The Vancouver Sun*, January 24, 2008.

Cooper, Glenda. "Convenient Technology Transforms Social Mores," *The Vancouver Sun*, December 8, 2012.

Cross, Gary S. *An All-Consuming Century: Why Commercialism Won in America* (New York: Columbia University Press, 2000).

Dedyna, Kathryn. "Workaholic 'Less Content with Life'," *The Vancouver Sun*, August 11, 2007.

Doyle, Alister. "Earth Losing 3 Species a Day, UN Says," *The Vancouver Sun*, May 23, 2007.

Drury, Jim. "Oceans' Rising Acid Levels Threaten Sea Life," *The Vancouver Sun*, August 8, 2012.

Dundes, Alan, ed. *Every Man His Way: Readings in Cultural Anthropology* (Englewood Cliffs, New Jersey: Prentice-Hall, 1968).

"Earth Could Warm by More Than 3.5 C, Leading to Extreme Weather: Research," *The Vancouver Sun*, May 25, 2012.

Fortado, Lindsay, Gavin Finch, and Liam Vaughan. "UBS's Rigging Fines Soar," *The Province*, December 20, 2012.

Fralic, Shelley. "Can't Change a Tire or Sew on a Button? When Did We Become So Helpless?" *The Vancouver Sun*, May 2, 2012.

Gentle, Douglas A., and Craig A. Anderson. *Media Violence and Children,* Chapter 7, "Violent Video Games: The Newest Media Violence Hazard" (Westport, Connecticut: Praeger, 2003).

His Holiness the Dalai Lama. *Ancient Wisdom, Modern World* (London: Abacus, 2006).

Huessmann, L. Rowell, Jessica Mosie-Titus, Cheryl-Lynn Podolski, and Leonard D. Eron, University of Michigan. "Longitudinal relations between children's exposure to TV violence and their aggressive and violent behavior in young adulthood: 1977–1992," *Developmental Psychology*, 2003, Vol. 39, No. 2.

"Internet Outpacing TV for Time Spent: TV Viewing Losing Ground," posted February 19, 2008.

Goleman, Daniel. *Social Intelligence: The New Science of Human Relationships* (New York: Bantam Dell, 2006).

Gray, Louise. "World's Population May Double by 2100, UN Warns," *The Vancouver Sun*, October 27, 2011.

"Greenhouse Gas Beats Ancient Threshold," *The Vancouver Sun*, May 11, 2013.

Greil, Anita, and Marta Falconi. "Former UBS Official, Now Regulator, in Spotlight," *The Wall Street Journal*, December 20, 2012.

Guest editorial from *Daily Telegraph*, "The Entire Global Trading System at Risk of Collapse," *The Vancouver Sun*, October 13, 2011.

Harris, Misty. "Canadians Dependent on Smartphones: Survey," *The Vancouver Sun*, December 27, 2012.

Heaven, Pamela. "Repeat of 1931 on Horizon: Economists," *The Vancouver Sun*, June 27, 2012.

Helin, Calvin. *The Economic Dependency Trap: Breaking Free to Self-Reliance* (St. Louis: Ravencrest Publishing, 2011).

Highfield, Roger. "Virtual Worlds 'Could Replace Real Relationships'," *The Telegraph*, June 19, 2007.

Jackson, Tim, and Peter Victor. "Prosperity without Growth Is Possible," *The Vancouver Sun*, September 19, 2011, A11.

Jan, Mark Williams, Alan Smith, et al. "Are We Now Living in the Anthropocene?" *GSA Today*, 18, No. 2 (February 2008).

Keith, David. "America's Fatal Addiction to Prescription Drugs," *The Guardian*, June 20, 2011.

Kielburger, Craig, and Marc Kielburger. *Me to We: Turning Self-Help on Its Head* (Mississauga: John Wiley & Sons, Canada, 2004).

Klinenberg, Eric. "Solo nation: American consumers stay single," CNNMoney, January 25, 2012.

Korten, David C. *The Post-Corporate World: Life after Capitalism* (San Francisco: Berrett-Koehler, 1999).

Kroeber, Theodora. *Ishi in Two Worlds* (Berkeley: University of California Press, 2002, 2004; originally published in 1961).

Lee, Jung Young. *The Principle of Changes: Understanding the I Ching* (New York: University Books, 1971).

Leggett, Jeremy. "Prosperity without Growth: Economics for a Finite Planet by Tim Jackson," *The Guardian*, January 23, 2010.

Lemonick, Michael D. "CO2 Hit Record High in 2011—UN Report," *The Guardian*, November 20, 2012.

Le Roux, Marriette. "Working Cooperatively Led to Bigger Brain Size, Study Suggests," *The Vancouver Sun*, April 11, 2012.

"Libor Stands for London Interbank Offered Rate. Bank CEO Faces Pressure to Resign as Inquiry Launched," *The Vancouver Sun*, July 3, 2012.

Liptak, Adam. "U.S. Prison Population Dwarfs That of Other Nations," *The New York Times*, April 23, 2008.

"Living standards to fall, OECD warns," *Vancouver Sun*, March 16, 2012.

Louv, Richard. *Last Child in the Woods* (Algonquin Books of Chapel Hill: New York, 2005).

Manthorpe, Jonathan. "HSBC Struggles with Serving Higher Power and Earthly Demands," *The Vancouver Sun*, August 7, 2012.

Marche, Stephen. "Is Facebook Making Us Lonely?" *The Atlantic*, May 2012.

Marsden, William. "Humans Usher in Risky Age of Man," *The Vancouver Sun*, January 30, 2012.

McLuhan, Marshall. *Understanding Media: The Extensions of Man*, 2nd ed. (New York: McGraw-Hill Book Company, 1964).

Miner, Horace. "Body Ritual among the Nacirema," *The American Anthropologist*, Vol. 58, Issue 3, 1956, 503–07.

"More Than 16,300 Creatures Listed as At Risk of Extinction," *The Vancouver Sun*, September 13, 2007.

Mott, Maryann. "Did Animals Sense the Tsunami Was Coming?" *National Geographic News*, January 4, 2005.

Munro, Margaret. "Humanity 'Must Do More with Less'," *The Vancouver Sun*, May 13, 2011.

Mustoe, Howard and Svenja O'Donnell. "Top Barclays Execs Resign Amid Scandal," *The Vancouver Sun*, July 4, 2012.

Myers, David G. *Psychology* (New York: Worth Publishers, 2003), 338–39.

Neihardt, John G. *Black Elk Speaks* (New York: Excelsior Editions, 2008).

"Oceans Getting Acidic at Unprecedented Rate," *The Vancouver Sun*, March 2, 2012.

Pandurangi, Ashvin. "Our Depraved Future of Debt Slavery (Part I)," February 23, 2012.

Partnoy, Frank, and Jesse Etinger. "What's inside America's banks?" *The Atlantic*, January/February 2013.

Pearlman, Jonathan. "Mining Magnate Is World's Richest Woman," *The Vancouver Sun*, May 26, 2012, B8.

Perreaux, Les. "A Mystery: Why Jean Charest Chose to Blink the First Time Out," *The Globe and Mail*, June 2, 2012, F6.

Phillips, Jack. "World Needs Vegetarian Diet by 2050, Says Report," *Epoch Times*, August–September 5, 2012.

Pickover, Clifford A. *Time: A Traveler's Guide* (New York: Oxford University Press, 1998).

Pylas, Pan and Pete Yost. "HSBC to Pay $1.9-Billion Fine," *The Vancouver Sun*, December 12, 2012.

Rowbotham, Michael. *The Grip of Death: A Study of Modern Money, Debt Slavery and Destructive Economics* (Charlbury, UK: Jon Carpenter Publishing, 2009).

Sandel, Michael J. "What Isn't for Sale?" *The Atlantic*, April 2012.

Sanford, Katherine. "Losses for Words," *Up Here*, 24, No. 3 (April–May, 2008).

Savage, Luiza Ch. "Rescue Operation: Can the Canada Pension Fund Save the American Social Security System?" *Maclean's,* June 18, 2007.

Schopmeyer, Kim D., and Bradley J. Fisher. "Insiders and Outsiders: Exploring Ethnocentrism and Cultural Relativity in Sociology Courses," *Teaching Sociology,* Vol. 21, 1993 (April: 148–53).

Schor, Juliet B. *Plenitude* (New York: The Penguin Press, 2010).

Silesius, Angelus translated, introduced, and drawn by Fredrick Franck. *Messenger of the Heart: The Book of Angelus Silesius* (Bloomington, Indiana: World Wisdom Inc., 2005).

Simpson, Scott. "Global Effort Needed to Avoid Environmental Disaster," *The Vancouver Sun*, November 17, 2007.

Simpson, Scott. "Tough Fossil Fuel Curbs Urged," *The Vancouver Sun*, November 7, 2007.

Slade, Giles. *Made to Break: Technology and Obsolescence in America* (Cambridge, MA: Harvard University Press, 2006).

Spencer, Richard. "China's Pollution Death Toll Revealed: 750,00 a Year," *The Vancouver Sun*.

Squires, Nick. "Drought Leads Australians to Seek Ancient Aboriginal Solutions," *The Vancouver Sun*, May 5, 2007, A12.

"Students Lose Sense of Self When Unplugged," *The Vancouver Sun*, April 2, 2011.

Sykes, J. B., ed. *The Concise Oxford Dictionary*, 7th ed. (New York: Oxford University Press, 1984).

Tanphanich, Alisa. "U.S. TV Time Far Exceeds Time Spent on Exercise," *The Daily Californian*, Wednesday, March 31, 2004.

The Associated Press, "Rich Countries Are Not the Happiest," *The Province*, December 20, 2012.

Tippet, Krista (contributor). *Einstein's God: Conversation about Science and the Human Spirit* (New York: Penguin Group, 2006).

Twist, Lynne. *The Soul of Money: Transferring Your Relationship with Money and Life* (New York: W. W. Norton & Company, 2003).

Valiant, John. *The Golden Spruce: A Story of Madness and Greed* (Toronto, Ontario: Vintage Canada, 2005).

Vicini, James. "More Americans Behind Bars Than Ever," *The Vancouver Sun*, February 29, 2008.

"Washington State Presses for Action on Ocean Acidity," *The Vancouver Sun*, November 29, 2012.

Welch, Craig. "CO2 Eating Away at Marine Life Faster Than Expected: Scientists," *The Vancouver Sun*, March 7, 2012.

Wilkinson, Richard, and Kate Pickett. *The Spirit Level: Why Equality Is Good for Everyone* (London: Penguin Books, 2010).

Yen, Hope. Associated Press, "Revised Government Formula Shows New Poverty High: 49.1M," November 7, 2011.

Zabarenko, Deborah. "Heat Could Kill 150,000 in U.S. Cities This Century," *Vancouver Sun*, May 25, 2012.

Online Sources

"25 People to Blame for the Financial Crisis," *Time*. http://www.time.com/time/specials/packages/article/0,28804,1877351_1877350_1877331,00.html.

2007 Social Security Trustees Report. http://72.14.253.104/search?q=cache:giPshMUt ZtAJ:budget.senate.gov/democratic/charts/2007/Hearings/packet_Healthpercent 2520Care_Orszag_062107.pdf+long-term+budget+shortfall+david+walker+2007& hl=en&ct=clnk&cd=4.

Ahmed, Kamal, and Jonathan Wynne-Jones. "Suicide of Deloitte Partner Daniel Pirron Linked to Standard Chartered's Iran Scandal," *The Telegraph*, August 22, 2012. http://www.telegraph.co.uk/finance/newsbysector/banksandfinance/9484442/ Suicide-of-Deloitte-partner-Daniel-Pirron-linked-to-Standard Chartereds-Iran-scandal.html.

Amadeo, Kimberly. "What are the components of GDP?" http://useconomy.about.com/ od/grossdomesticproduct/f/GDP_Components.htm.

American Psychological Association. "Stress in America." http://www.apa.org/news/press/ releases/stress/key-findings.aspx.

American Psychological Association. "Substance Abuse: The Nation's Number One Health Problem, But There Is Hope," June 2001, Vol. 32, No. 6. http://www.apa. org/monitor/jun01/subabuseone.aspx.

"Americans Were 'Living in a Fool's Paradise' That's Gone Forever, George Soros," http:// finance.yahoo.com/tech-ticker/article/228536/Americans-Were-percent22Living-in-a-Foolpercent27s-Paradisepercent22-Thatpercent27s-Gone-Forever-Soros-Says? tickers=^DJI,^GSPC,SPY,DIA,QQQQ,TLT; http://thesurvivalpodcast.com/forum/ index.php?topic=4702.0

Anita. "Private consumption share of GDP expected to jump in China by 2015: Economist," *Global Times*, March 23, 2011. http://en.trade2cn.com/dataservice/ 110323155005n73-1.html

"Asia-Pacific Poised to Dominate North America as World's Top Ad Market, According to 'Most Comprehensive' Edition of the eMarketer Global Media Intelligence Report," October 10, 2012. http://www.emarketer.com/newsroom/index.php/asiapacific-poiseddominate-north-america-worlds-top-ad-market-comprehensive-edition-emarketerglobal-media-intelligence-report.

Baily, Martin N., and Susan Lund. "American Hangover," *The International Economy* (Summer 2009), 24. http://www.international-economy.com/TIE_Su09_BailyLund.pdf.

Beard, Charles. *The Rise of American Civilisation* (London, J. Cape, 1927). http://www. monticello.org/site/jefferson/private-banks-quotation and http://www.markturner. net/2008/10/02/jeffersons-bogus-bank-quote-in-the-wild.

Beucke, Dan. "Timely retirements, outrageous bonuses, and other epic executive handouts," *Bloomberg Businessweek*, December 21, 2011. http://www.businessweek. com/finance/occupy-wall-street/archives/2011/12/timely_retirements_outrageous_ bonuses_and_other_epic_corporate_handouts.html.

Black Elk. Originally from *The Sacred Pipe*. http://www.rodneyohebsion.com/native american-proverbs-quotes.htm#religions.

Brit, Robert Roy. "Universe Measured: We're 156 Billion Light-years Wide!" CNN.com, May 24, 2004. http://www.cnn.com/2004/TECH/space/05/24/universe.wide/ index.html.

Buchanan, Patrick. "The Trade Issue Is Back, Big-Time," March 4, 2008, from Web site Real Clear Politics. http://www.realclearpolitics.com/articles/2008/03/the_second_battle_of_nafta.html.

Buffalo Field Campaign. http://www.buffalofieldcampaign.org/aboutbuffalo/bisonnative americans.html.

Butler, Eamon. "The Morality of Capitalism," October 23, 2011. http://www.adamsmith.org/blog/tax-and-economy/the-morality-of-capitalism.

Cherry, Kendra. "Loneliness." http://psychology.about.com/od/psychotherapy/a/loneliness.htm.

"China's Under-Consumption Over Stated," Finfacts Ireland Web site, September 16, 2009. http://www.finfacts.ie/irishfinancenews/article_1017904.shtml.

"China's consumption challenge," *The European Business Review.* http://www.europeanbusinessreview.com/?p=1195.

Clugston, Chris. "Excessive Consumption—America's Real Addiction," October 20, 2007. http://www.culturechange.org/cms/index.php?option=com_content&task=view&id=128 &Itemid=1.

"Compiled by TV-Free America," 1322 18th Street, NW, Washington, D.C. 20036. http://quotes.dictionary.com/it_is_a_medium_of_entertainment_which_permits.

Corwin, Jeff. "The Sixth Extinction," *Los Angeles Times,* November 30, 2009. http://articles.latimes.com/2009/nov/30/opinion/la-oe-corwin30-2009nov30.

"Despite High Profits HSBC Puts Aside Billions for Money Laundering Fines," *RT,* July 30, 2012. http://rt.com/business/news/hsbc-money-laundering-billion-375.

Dobbs, Richard. "Unleashing the Chinese Consumer," *Newsweek International,* September 5, 2009. http://www.mckinsey.com/Insights/MGI/In_the_news/Unleashing_the_Chinese_Consumer.

Dobbs, Richard, Andrew Grant, and Jonathan Woetsel. "Unleashing the Chinese Consumer," McKinsey Global Institute, September 5, 2009. http://www.mckinsey.com/Insights/MGI/In_the_news/Unleashing_the_Chinese_consumer.

Doherty, Greg. "Joseph Campbell's Four Functions of Mythology." http://drake.marin.k12.ca.us/staff/doherty/fourfunctionsmythology.html.

Eaglesham, Jean, and Evan Perez. "UBS Let Off Too Easy, Critics Say," *The Wall Street Journal,* December 21, 2012. http://online.wsj.com/article/SB10001424127887324731304578191801981480008.html.

Editorial, "Lessons from the London Whale," *The New York Times Sunday Review,* January 20, 2013, 10. http://www.nytimes.com/2013/01/20/opinion/sunday/lessons-from-the-londonwhale.html?_r=0.

Erler, Alexandre. "Should we be afraid of virtual reality?" http://www.practicalethicsnews.com/practicalethics/2009/09/should-we-be-afraid-of-virtual-reality.html.

Fellner, James. "US Addiction to Incarceration Puts 2.3 Million in Prison," December 1, 2006. http://hrw.org/english/docs/2006/12/01/usdom14728.htm.

Fellner, Jamie. "Millions of Americans in Denial about Their Own Drug Abuse," http://www.drug-addiction.com/drugs_and_denial.htm.

Galbraith, John Kenneth. *Money: Whence It Came, Where It Went* (Boston: Houghton-Mifflin, 1975). http://www.legalforgery.com/pages/detail.php?section=27&id=152.

Guo, Kai, and Papa N'Diaye, "Determinants of China's Private Consumption: An International Perspective," IMF Working Paper, WP/10/93, April 2010. https://docs.google.com/viewer?a=v&q=cache:zRAeEPA_NHkJ:www.reloo ney.info/SI_FAOAsia/China_300.pdf+consumption+percent+of+gdp&hl=en &gl=ca&pid=bl&srcid=ADGEESgvlHHNn1TqjENUvmWb0 GmChBCzDEmRslWRCwIxZ8Bu0hq7cLrvp-B5PKKNVabY5rH6VN4y-pQ JZSFHlK3PtjS3oconeid8bpSDypzdBFqx5beQTygUSGv267As 33ob9W5n5Qn&sig=AHIEtbTcvBWaeBQ3_xyhUT_GB4XXNSUYEw.

Heinberg, Richard. *The End of Growth: Adapting to Our New Economic Reality* (Gabriola Island, BC: New Society Publishers, 2011). http://www.amazon.ca/End-Growth-Adapting-Economic-Reality/dp/0865716951#reader_0865716951.

Husten, Larry. "The grim impact of living alone," *Forbes*, June 18, 2012. http://www.for bes.com/sites/larryhusten/2012/06/18/the-grim-impact-of-loneliness-and-living-alone.

Kage, Ben. "United States Imprisons More People Than China, Russia or Any Other Nation, Experts Say," NaturalNews.com, December 13, 2006. http://www.natural news.com/021290.html.

Kennedy, Robert F. "Remarks at the University of Kansas," March 18, 1968. http://www. poli-sci.utah.edu/~dlevin/AmPolTho/RFK@Kansas.pdf.

"Loneliness is getting rampant in America," Softpedia. http://news.softpedia.com/news/ Loneliness-Is-Getting-Rampant-in-America-27518.shtml.

Miedma, Doug, and Lauren Tara Lacpra. "Outgoing Exec Rips Goldman Sachs," *The Vancouver Sun*, March 15, 2012. http://www.vancouversun.com/sports/Outgoing+ exec+rips+Goldman+Sachs/6305703/story.html.

PBS series, *The Power of Myth*. http://video.pbs.org/video/2201676017.

Pearman, Court. "Can the World Support an American Lifestyle?" *Epoch Times*, February 17, 2007, 6. http://en.epochtimes.com/news/7-2-12/51604.html.

Peck, Don. "Can the Middle Class Be Saved?" *The Atlantic*, September 2011, 62. http:// www.stwr.org/poverty-inequality/key-facts.html.

"Perception of Time Pressure Impairs Performance," *Science Daily*, February 16, 2009.

Perry, Geraldine, and Ken Fousek. *The Two Faces of Money* (Shelbyville, KY: Wasteland Press, 2007). http://www.thetwofacesofmoney.com/files/money.pdf.

Rappaport, Liz. "Banks Settles Iran Money Case," *The Wall Street Journal*, August 15, 2012. http://online.wsj.com/article/SB1000087239639044431810457758938042755942 6.html.

"RBS Probed by U.S. Over Alleged Iran Sanction Violations—Report," *Mail* Online, August 22, 2012. http://www.dailymail.co.uk/news/article-2191878/RBS-probed-U-Salleged-Iran-sanction-violations-says-report.html.

Sample, Ian. "Yangtze River Dolphin Driven to Extinction," *Guardian Unlimited*, August 16, 2007. http://www.guardian.co.uk/environment/2007/aug/08/endangered-species.conservation.

Shapiro, Mark. September 5, 2000. http://www.simulconference.com/clients/sowf/interviews/interview3.html or http://en.wikiquote.org/wiki/George_Soros.

Sheridan, Samuel. "Putting China's low household consumption in perspective," World Economic Roundtable, March 15, 2011. http://roundtable.newamerica.net/blog posts/2011/putting_china_s_low_household_consumption_in_perspective-46600.

Smith, Adam. *An Inquiry into the Nature and Causes of the Wealth of Nations*, Book 1, Chapter 2, 1776. http://geolib.com/smith.adam/won1-02.html.

Social Security System?" *Maclean's* magazine, June 18, 2007. http://www.macleans.ca/article.jsp?content=20070618_106225_106225.

"Standard Chartered Settles Iran Money Laundering Charges," August 14, 2011. http://www.usatoday.com/money/industries/banking/story/2012-08-14/standardchartered-iran-money-laundering-settlement/57052122/1.

Steiner, Rudolf. "Man's Position in the Cosmic Whole, the Platonic World-Year," Dornach, January 28, 1917, GA 174, published in *Anthroposophic News Sheet*, Nos. 1–2 (January 1940). http://wn.rsarchive.org/Lectures/ManPos_index.html.

Swartz, Spencer, and Shai Oster. "China Tops U.S. in Energy Use," *The Wall Street Journal*, July 19, 2010. http://online.wsj.com/article/NA_WSJ_PUB:SB10001424052748703720504575376712353150310.html.

"The Cost of Pollution in China." http://web.worldbank.org/WBSITE/EXTERNAL/COUNTRIES/EASTASIAPACIFICEXT/EXTEAPREGTOPENVIRONMENT/0,,contentMDK:21252897~pagePK:34004173~piPK:34003707~theSitePK:502886,00.html.

"The Melting North," special report. *The Economist*, June 16, 2012, 3. http://www.economist.com/node/21556798.

Thomas, Lyn. "Student Reactions to Horace Miner's Body Ritual Among the Nacirema." http://www.anthropology.pomona.edu/html/Faculty/lthomas/Thomas_1994-Body Ritual.pdf.

"Time: A Traveller's Guide," 12. http://bit.ly/AtPIXV.

Toft, Klaus (producer). ABC documentary *Killers in Eden*. http://www.killersofeden.com.

"Twenty Percent of Americans Risk Prescription Drug Addiction for Non-Medical Reasons," January 29, 2012. http://blog.drugrehabreferral.com/views/2012/01/29/twenty-percent-of-americans-risk-prescription-drug-addiction-for-non-medical-reasons.

United Nations. "World Population to 2300," Department of Economic and Social Affairs, Population Division, New York, 2004. http://www.un.org/esa/population/publications/longrange2/WorldPop2300final.pdf.

Wehrein, Peter, ed. "Astounding Increase in Antidepressant Use by Americans," *Harvard Health Publications* (October 20, 2011). http://www.health.harvard.edu/blog/astounding-increase-in-antidepressant-use-by-americans-201110203624.

Wells, Cheryl. "Suns, Moons, Clocks, and Bells: Native Americans and Time," University of Wyoming, Department of History, December 1, 2008, 1. http://www-bcf.usc.edu/~philipje/USC_History_Seminar/Wells/Wells_SUNS_MOONS_reading.pdf.

Woods, Sarah. "Horses Have a Sixth Sense to Pick Up on Anxiety, Research Has Shown," *Horse & Hound*, July 17, 2009.

Yen, Hope. Associated Press, Article on 2010 census data titled "Census Finds Record Gap Between Rich and Poor," September 28, 2010.

http://1020isawesome.pbworks.com/w/page/4732848/Reading%20Response%2013.

http://academic.udayton.edu/RondaScantlin/CMM449_Fall2003/Comm449_Fall/3_Topic3/Media_Violence_March2003.pdf.

http://animaluniversity.com/2010/do-horses-have-a-sixth-sense.

http://archive.dailycal.org/printable.php?id=14717.

http://au.answers.yahoo.com/answers2/frontend.php/question?qid=20080306101717AAXyESH.

http://bit.ly/A3IoMp.

http://blogs.discovery.com/animal_oddities/2011/03/can-animals-sense-earthquakes-and-tsunamis.html.

http://books.google.ca/books?id=4eRL24p4uwkC&printsec=frontcover&source=gbs_ge_summary_r&cad=0#v=onepage&q&f=false.

http://books.google.ca/books?id=zmBPI4aakLAC&pg=PA39&dq=Time+is+of+your+own+making+silesius&hl=en&sa=X&ei=y2YYUbSLFMbOiwKzhYG4DA&ved=0CC4Q6AEwAA#v=onepage&q=Time%20is%20of%20your%20own%20making%20silesius&f=false or http://www.notable-quotes.com/t/time_quotes.html.

http://chinese.yabla.com/chinese-english-pinyin-dictionary.php?define=xiaokang.

http://cmp.hku.hk/2007/09/19/622.

http://www.csun.edu/science/health/docs/tv&health.html.

http://duca94.wordpress.com/2011/05/22/reading-review-body-ritual-amongthe-nacirema.

http://en.wikipedia.org/wiki/It_Takes_a_Village.

http://en.wikipedia.org/wiki/JAK_Members_Bank.

http://en.wikipedia.org/wiki/Local_exchange_trading_system.

http://en.wikipedia.org/wiki/Time.

http://en.wikipedia.org/wiki/Xiaokang.

http://en.wikiquote.org/wiki/Xun_zi

http://examiner-enterprise.com/sections/news/world/revised-government-formula-shows-newpoverty-high-491m.html.

http://indurhedgefund.blogspot.ca/2009/04/americans-were-living-in-fools-paradise.html.

http://www.jacksonkatz.com/PDF/ChildrenMedia.pdf.

http://myweb.cwpost.liu.edu/paievoli/finals/505Sp_03/Prj1/irene_piechota.htm.

http://news.nationalgeographic.com/news/2002/06/0627_020628_wadedavis.html.

http://news.yahoo.com/revised-govt-formula-shows-poverty-high-49-1m-135427317.html.

http://offoxesandhedgehogs.wordpress.com/2012/01/29/rituals-of-the-nacire mamust-read-article-before-summaries-underneath.

http://onlinelibrary.wiley.com/doi/10.1525/aa.1956.58.3.02a00080/abstract.

http://people.hsc.edu/faculty-staff/maryp/Core/homo_erectus_to_homo_sapiens.htm.

http://quotationsbook.com/quote/9484.

http://quotationsbook.com/quote/26811.

http://rescomp.stanford.edu/~cheshire/EinsteinQuotes.html.

http://roundtable.newamerica.net/sites/newamerica.net/files/articles/Slide2.PNG.

http://roundtable.newamerica.net/sites/newamerica.net/files/articles/Slide4.PNG.

http://rprogress.org/index.htm.

http://science.howstuffworks.com/environmental/life/zoology/all-aboutanimals/pet-sixth-sense1.htm.

http://thinkexist.com/quotations/arrogance/2.html.

http://thinkexist.com/quotations/technology.

http://wiki.answers.com/Q/Who_said_A_society_is_measured_by_how_it_treats_its_weakest_members.

http://www.aacap.org/cs/root/developmentor/the_impact_of_media_violence_on_children_and_adolescents_opportunities_for_clinical_interventions.

http://www.aafp.org/online/en/home/policy/policies/v/violencemedia.html.

http://www.amazon.com/o/ASIN/0393050971/ref=nosim/thesoulofmone-20#reader_0393050971.

http://www.afriprov.org/index.php/african-proverb-of-the-month/23-1998pro verbs/137-november-1998-proverb.html.

http://www.alleyinsider.com/2007/08/ibm-survey-time.html. See also: Mike Sachoff.

http://www.arkanimals.com/dlg/tsunami_earthquake_animal_prediction.htm.

http://www.bbhq.com/bomrstat.htm.

http://www.birdnote.org/birdnote-transcript.cfm?id=767.

http://www.berkeley.edu/news/media/releases/96legacy/releases.96/14310.html.

http://www.bloomberg.com/news/2011-10-13/growing-income-divide-may-increase-u-s-vulnerability-to-financial-crises.html.

http://www.bom.gov.au/iwk.

http://www.brainyquote.com/quotes/keywords/abyss.html.

http://www.brainyquote.com/quotes/quotes/a/abrahamlin103270.html.

http://www.brainyquote.com/quotes/authors/c/charles_darwin.html.

http://www.brainyquote.com/quotes/quotes/g/geoffreych165940.html.

http://www.brainyquote.com/quotes/keywords/growth.html.

http://www.brainyquote.com/quotes/keywords/ritual.html.

http://www.canada.com/story.html?id=c7380cc2-12a7-4327-955c-8b224164c50d.

http://www.canada.com/vancouversun/news/story.html?id=b262e8d9-800c-49ec-966f-4d71577c9a9a, http://www.webmd.com/balance/stress-management/news/20121018/stress-parents-obesity-kids.

http://www.cbpp.org/cms/?fa=view&id=3220.

http://www.cnn.com/2008/HEALTH/conditions/10/07/economic.stress/index.html.

http://dictionary.reference.com/browse/myth.

http://www.csun.edu/science/health/docs/tv&health.html.

http://drronbittle.com/custom_content/c_181600_1_stress_reliever_revealed.html.

http://www.ecoknow.ca/articles/awr_01.pdf.

http://www.econlib.org/library/Smith/smMS.html.

http://www.econlib.org/library/Smith/smWN.html.

http://www.efmoody.com/miscellaneous/loneliness.html.

http://www.equalitytrust.org.uk/.

http://www.feasta.org/documents/review2/carrie2.htm.

http://finance.fortune.cnn.com/2012/01/25/eric-klinenberg-going-solo.

http://www.foxnews.com/story/0,2933,143737,00.html.

http://www.futureofuschinatrade.com/fact/us-china-trade-data-household-consumption-share-of-GDP.

http://www.goodreads.com/quotes/tag/oneness.

http://www.gsajournals.org/perlserv/?request=get-toc&issn=1052-5173&volume=18&issue=2.

http://www.guardian.co.uk/commentisfree/2011/sep/05/punishmentrioters-help.

http://www.guardian.co.uk/books/2010/jan/23/prosperity-without-growth-timjackson.

http://www.guardian.co.uk/commentisfree/cifamerica/2011/jun/10/prescription drug-abuse.

http://www.guardian.co.uk/environment/2012/nov/20/co2-record-high-2011-unreport.

http://www.horseandhound.co.uk/news/397/286372.html.

http://www.indigenouspeople.net/quotes.htm.

http://www.jstor.org/pss/1318635.

http://www.kidcyber.com.au/topics/dino_eras.htm.

http://www.lets-linkup.com.

http://www.letslinkuk.net.

http://www.livinglifefully.com/nativeamericanwisdom.htm.

http://www.marketoracle.co.uk/Article33279.html.

http://www.medicalnewstoday.com.

http://www.medscape.org/viewarticle/562721.

http://www.merriam-webster.com/dictionary/atomistic.

http://www.merriam-webster.com/dictionary/baleen percent20whale.

https://www.msu.edu/~jdowell/miner.html?pagewanted=al.

http://www.naturalwellnesscare.com/stress-statistics.html.

http://news.nationalgeographic.com/news/2005/01/0104_050104_tsunami_animals. html.

http://www.nytimes.com/2008/04/23/world/americas/23iht-23prison.12253738.html? pagewanted=all.

http://www.operationmorningstar.org/Americanpercent20Indianpercent20Historypercent20 Overview.htm.

http://oxforddictionaries.com/definition/english/ritual.

http://www.pbs.org/wnet/nature/episodes/killers-in-eden/introduction/1048.

http://www.pembina.org/pub/58.

http://www.practicalethicsnews.com/practicalethics/2009/09/should-we-be-afraidof-virtual-reality.html.

http://www.praxistech.com.

http://psychcentral.com/news/2010/09/05/chronic-social-stress-linked-to-obesity/17685.html.

http://psychology.about.com/od/nindex/g/needtobelong.htm.

http://www.psychology.iastate edu/faculty/caa/abstracts/2000-2004/03GA.pdf.

http://www.quotecosmos.com/subjects/170/Ceremony.

http://www.quoteworld.org/quotes/4101.

http://www.royalroads.ca/rrunews/greening-china.

http://www.salon.com/2010/09/28/us_census_recession_s_impact_1.

http://www.sciencedaily.com/releases/2009/02/090210162035.htm.

http://www.searchquotes.com/quotation/I_am_sorry_to_say_that_there_is_too_much_point_to_the_wisecrack_that_life_is_extinct_on_other_planet/3010.

http://www.soulofmoney.org/about/about-the-book.

http://www.spiritbearyouth.org.

http://www.studymode.com/subjects/nacirema-page1.html.

http://www.telegraph.co.uk/news/uknews/1554999/Virtual-worlds-could-replacereal-relationships.html.

http://technology.timesonline.co.uk/tol/news/tech_and_web/the_web/article5139532.ece.

http://www.theatlantic.com/magazine/archive/2012/04/what-isnt-for-sale/308902.

http://www.thefreedictionary.com/atomistic.

http://www.thegoddards.ca/alexgoddardblog/?p=1066.

http://www.theorderoftime.com/science/galactic.html.

http://thinkexist.com/quotes/with/keyword/american_language.

http://www.time.com/time/specials/packages/article/0,28804,2101745_2102132_2102373-2,00.html.

http://www.trivia-library.com/a/36th-us-president-lyndon-b-johnson.htm.

http://www.usdebtclock.org. Figures from February 7, 2013.

http://www.webpronews.com/topnews/2008/02/19/internet-outpacing-tv-for-timespent.

http://www.well.com/~davidu/sixthextinction.html.

http://www.workaholics-anonymous.org/page.php?page=signposts.

http://www.worldprayers.org/archive/prayers/meditations/i_do_not_think_that.html.

http://www.youtube.com/watch?v=aW2pj109Cr8.

http://www1.american.edu/ted/ice/buffalo.htm.

http://www2.canada.com/saskatoonstarphoenix/news/business/story.html?id=7dd673
54-73ca-4133-a73d-69cce3f0543c&p=1.

http://www2.canada.com/vancouversun/news/archives/story.html?id=11c3d
fcac0b5-4e16-b285-b6748bd16a39.

http://www2.canada.com/vancouversun/news/archives/story.html?id=408221a1-
8eef-4503-b318-1f8c973b0570.

http://www2.canada.com/vancouversun/news/archives/story.html?id=b73a171a-
39fb-4685-ab40-d378644332e9.

INDEX

Note: Page numbers with *f* indicate figures.

A

Abbey, Edward, 15
ABN Amro Bank, 49
A.C. Nielsen Co., 74
Addams, Jane, 143
Aesop's Fables as social myth, 151
American Anthropologist, 83
American ethnocentrism, 81–88
  cultural legacy, saving, 84–88
  culture and, 82–84
  overview of, 81–82
American Psychological Association,
  34, 75
Ammons, A. R., 67
Anielski, Mark, 102–3, 107
Anthropocene era, 45
Apotheker, Léo, 49
Aquinas, Thomas, 102
Arab Spring, 97, 114, 115
Atlantic, The, 146
Atomistic views, 59–61, 61*f*
Aziz, Tariq, 97

B

Baiji dolphin, 43
Bank created debt, 15–19, 17*f,* 19–20*f*
Bank of England, 16, 17, 49–50
Bank of International Settlements, 16
Barclays Bank, 48

Barry, Dave, 81
Beecher, Henry Ward, 47
Behaviors, new technology and,
  72–73
Belonging, importance of, 135–39, 138*f*
Bergerac, Cyrano de, 63
Berreby, David, 133–34, 136
Beston, Henry, 126
Bierce, Ambrose, 121
Big Elk, 86
Black Elk, 59, 162
Board of Governors, 21
"Body Ritual among the Nacirema"
  (Miner), 83
Boomerang effect, loans and, 17
Boulding, Elise, 42
Boulding, Kenneth, 112
Boxing Day, 8–9
Branson, Mark, 48
Brazil, consumption in, 29*f*
Briggs, John, 60
Brown, Fred, 145
Brown, Lester, 28
Bureau of Ethnology, 156

C

Cacioppo, John, 146
Campbell, Joseph, 149, 150, 151,
  152, 155

Ceremony
  defined, 154
  value of, 154–57
Chaucer, Geoffrey, 52
Chesterton, Gilbert K., 5
China
  consumption in, 28–29, 29f
  environment pressures in, 42
  incarceration rates in, 37, 37f
Churchill, Winston, 36
Clarke, Ken, 116
Clugston, Chris, 14
Cochise, 86
Coleridge, Samuel Taylor, 77
Common sense
  contemporary trends impact on,
    77–80
  defined, 77–78
  lack of, 78–80
Communal cooperation/interaction,
  144–45
Communities
  being part of, 143–47
  benefits of, 143–44
  communal cooperation/interaction
    and, 144–45
  government interference with, 145
  make-up of, 143
  modern-day, drawbacks of, 145
  reasons for, 144
  requirements for real, 146–47
  social media, 146
Comparative income gap, 35–38,
  36f, 37f

Composite Wealth Indicators, 107
Confucius, 102, 156
Consumer confidence, 15
Consumption, 8–14
  advertising spending and, 9
  in America, 8–9, 13
  in China, 28–29, 29f
  Clugston and excessive, 14
  as cultural mind-set, 9–10
  demographics and, 25, 27, 27f
  economic model and long term
    problem of, 12–13, 12f
  Gross Domestic Product and,
    10–13, 11f, 12f, 28–29, 29f
Copernicus, Nicolaus, 63
"Cosmic Balance," 90–91
Cosmological myths, 151
Cosmos, place of people in,
  63–65
Creative Mythology (Campbell), 151
Credit Suisse Group AG, 49
Crockett, Andrew, 16
Cultural legacy, saving, 84–88
Cultural mind-set
  fundamentals of American, 8
  time concept and, 51–56
Culture and American
  ethnocentrism, 82–84

D
Dalai Lama, 123
Dances with Dependency (Helin),
  64, 145
Darwin, Charles, 84, 111

Holocene era, 45
Homo sapiens, longevity of, 64*f*
Hoover, J. Edgar, 93
Hot cognition, 133
Howard, Jane, 133
HSBC, 49
Huie, Jonathan Lockwood, 51
Hu Jintao, 102
Human Development Index, 107
Human-kind map, 133–34
Humility, attitude of, 64, 65

I
IBM, 49, 74
I Ching, 60, 65, 82, 83, 159
Incarceration rates, 36–38, 37*f*
India, consumption in, 29*f*
Indian adoption, 139–40
Indian time, 52–54
ING Bank NV, 49
*Inquiry into the Nature of and Causes of
    Wealth of Nations, An* (Smith), 47
Isenberg, Eugene, 49
"Is Facebook Making Us Lonely?"
    (Marche), 146
Ishi, 157, 162–63
"Ishi's Prayer," 163–64

J
Jackson, Simon, 44–45, 44*f*
Jackson, Tim, 112
JAK Members Bank of Sweden, 99
Japan, consumption in, 29*f*
Jefferson, Thomas, 21

Johnson, Lyndon B., 93
Johnson, Samuel, 125
J.P. Morgan, 50

K
Keller, Helen, 82
Kennedy, John F., 35, 69
Kennedy, Robert, 13–14, 105
Kermode bear, 44
Keynes, John Maynard, 105, 111
Killers in Eden (documentary), 127
King, Mervyn, 49–50
Kinney, Mark, 98
Korten, David C., 17
Kuznets, Simon, 105

L
Laxgibuu, 127
Leakey, Richard, 46
Lee, Jung Young, 60, 68, 159
Lehman Brothers, 50
Lincoln, Abraham, 63
Ling, Richard, 72
Liquidity ratio, 17, 18
Local Exchange Transaction Systems
    (LETS), 99
Loneliness (Cacioppo), 146
Loneliness, experiencing, 137. *See
    also* Belonging, importance of
Louv, Richard, 75

M
Madoff, Bernie, 49
Mammon, 102

Peat, F. David, 60
Pension system, demographics
    impact on, 25, 27–28, 27*f*
*Plan B 2.0: Rescuing a Planet under
    Stress and a Civilization in
    Trouble* (Brown), 28
Plenitude (Schor), 119
Primal nature, embracing, 125–31
    overview of, 125–26
    species, connecting to other,
        126–31
    spiritual nature of humans and, 131
Proceedings of Royal Society B (British
    journal), 144
Psychological myths, 151

R
Raman, V. V., 68
Rationality and science, 67–70
Red Cloud, Chief, 8, 86, 103
Red Jacket, 86
Reform, ten commandments
    for, 118
Religion and science, 68–69
Religious/spiritual myths, 151
Reserve/asset ratio, 17, 18
Respect, 155
Rinehart, Gina, 114
Ritual
    benefits of, 155–56
    ceremony and, 154–57
    Confucius and, 156
    defined, 154
    self-identity and, 156

Roosevelt, Franklin D., 77
Rowbotham, Michael, 16, 17,
    31, 33
Royal Bank of Scotland, 49
Ruskin, John, 105
Russia
    consumption in, 29*f*
    incarceration rates in, 37, 37*f*

S
Sandburg, Carl, 51
Sandel, Michael J., 38, 39, 99
Schor, Juliet B., 119
Schumacher, E. F., 71, 101
Science
    rationality and, 67–70
    religion and, 68–69
Scott, Willard, 139
Scruton, Roger, 73–74
Seattle, Chief, 59, 86
Second Life, 73
Self-identity and ritual, 156
Self-interest, defined, 47
Sensei, 155
Sigyidm hana'a Su Dalx (Helin,
    Princess Verna), 128*f*
Silesius, Angelus, 53
Sitting Bull, 81, 86
Sixth sense, 125–26
Smith, Adam, 47, 50
Smith, Greg, 48
Smith, Jodi R. R., 72–73
Sm'ooygit Nees Nuugan Noos (Helin,
    Chief Barry), 128*f*

Tribal distinctions, making,
133–34
Tribal structures, 139–40, 140*f*
Twist, Lynne, 98
Twitter, 146

U
UBS AG, 48
Understanding Media: The Extensions
of Man (McLuhan), 71
United States
consumption in, 29*f*
debt *vs.* GDP in, 33, 33*f*
incarceration rates in, 36–38, 37*f*
trade deficit in, 25
Us and Them: Understanding Your
Tribal Mind (Berreby), 133

V
Victor, Peter, 112
Virtual reality, negative impacts of,
73–74
Vivekanada, Swami, 59

W
Wakas, 86
War of the Worlds, The (radio drama), 83
Wealth
Chinese society and, 102
Christianity teachings and, 101–2

Genuine Progress Indicator and,
106–7, 107*f*
Genuine Wealth and, 107–8
Greek word for, 101
Gross Domestic Product and,
105–6, 107*f,* 161
historical meaning of, 101–3
measurements of, 105–10
Old English meaning of, 101
"Weeping Willow Weeps," 58
We-feeling, 136
Welles, Orson, 83
Wen Jiabao, 102
White, Te Taru, 86, 87*f*
Wilde, Oscar, 86
Wiseman, Rosalind, 75
Wood, Josiah, 16
World Conservation Union, 43
World of Warcraft, 73

X
Xiaokang, 102
Xiaokang shehui, 102
Xun Zi, 149, 155

Y
Yangtze River dolphin, 43

Z
Zebrowski, George, 53